GLEANINGS

from

MARYLAND NEWSPAPERS

1786–1790

Robert W. Barnes

HERITAGE BOOKS
2011

HERITAGE BOOKS
AN IMPRINT OF HERITAGE BOOKS, INC.

Books, CDs, and more—Worldwide

For our listing of thousands of titles see our website
at
www.HeritageBooks.com

Published 2011 by
HERITAGE BOOKS, INC.
Publishing Division
100 Railroad Ave. #104
Westminster, Maryland 21157

Other Heritage Books by Robert W. Barnes
and Bettie Stirling Carothers

1783 Tax List of Baltimore County

Index of Baltimore County Wills, 1659–1850

Other Heritage Books by Robert W. Barnes:

Baltimore and Fell's Point Directory of 1796

Baltimore County, Marriage References, 1659–1746

Baltimore County, Maryland Deed Abstracts, 1659–1750

Gleanings from Maryland Newspapers, 1776–85

Gleanings from Maryland Newspapers, 1786–90

Gleanings from Maryland Newspapers, 1791–95

*Index to Marriages and Deaths in the
Baltimore County Advocate, 1850–1864*

International Standard Book Numbers
Paperbound: 978-0-7884-3403-7
Clothbound: 978-0-7884-8794-1

INTRODUCTION

Newspapers often contain helpful information for the genealogist. Not only deaths and marriages but personal notices also shed light on the life and activities of those fascinating people, our ancestors.

The gleanings in this volume, a companion to the author's GLEANINGS FROM MARYLAND NEWSPAPERS, 1776-1785, were taken from Maryland newspapers at the Enoch Pratt Free Library and the Maryland Historical Society in Baltimore. A few Maryland items were also taken from issues of the Pennsylvania Herald and York General Advertiser at the York County Historical Society in Pennsylvania. Deaths and marriages of Maryland inhabitants were abstracted as were notices concerning the settlement of estates, lost heirs who were sought, and eloping wives.

The entries are arranged in alphabetical order with the symbol for the newspaper used and the date of issue given in parentheses after the item. A full name index lists those people mentioned in notices of individuals with different surnames.

This volume is intended to complement and not duplicate the author's MARRIAGES AND DEATHS FROM THE MARYLAND GAZETTE, 1727-1839, published by the Genealogical Publishing Company, Baltimore.

The following is a list of newspapers used, with their abbreviations and the dates the newspaper is available.

AMG - (Annapolis) Maryland Gazette
    Both Pratt and the Maryland Historical Society have microfilm copies of the paper for 1786, 1787, 1788, 1789, and 1790.

BMG - Maryland Gazette or Baltimore General Advertiser
    Copies are at the Pratt or MHS for the entire period 1786 -1790.

BMJ - Maryland Journal and Baltimore Advertiser
    Copies exist for the entire period.

EMH - (Easton) Maryland Herald and Eastern Shore Intelligencer
    Microfilm copies at MHS begin with start of publication, 11 May 1790, and run for remainder of the year.

EWS - (Elizabeth-Town, Washington Co.) Washington Spy
    Microfilm copies beginning 26 Aug. 1790 are at the MHS.

FMC - (Frederick) Maryland Chronicle or Universal Advertiser
    Microfilm at MHS begins 18 Jan. 1786 and continues through 1787

YPH - Pennsylvania Herald and York General Advertiser
    Copies at York Co. Hist. Soc. cover the period 1789 - 1790.

GLEANINGS FROM MARYLAND NEWSPAPERS

1786 -- 1790

ADAMS, Doctor, son of the Honorable Samuel Adams, died at Boston the week of the
    18th inst. "New York, Jan. 29" (BMJ, 8 Feb. 1788)

ADAMS, Samuel, teacher of languages, married Mrs. Thomson, widow of the late
    Andrew Thomson. (BMJ, 29 May 1789)

ADDISON, Rev. Henry, died Monday, 31st ult., at his seat in Prince Georges
    County. (BMG, 8 Sept. 1789)

AITKEN, Robert, Jr., printer, and Ann Pearson, both of Philadelphia, were married
    there on Thursday, 9th inst. (FMC, 29 April 1787)

ALBOY, Capt. Richard, late of New York, deceased; Samuel Dodge of Fells Point,
    Baltimore, will settle the estate. (BMG, 26 Dec. 1786)

ALLERTON, Robert, a blacksmith by trade, born in England, supposed to have lived
    in Annapolis since about Feb. 1771, should apply to the printer. (BMG, 24
    April 1787)

ALLISON, Col. John, and Rebecca, daughter of Robert McCrea of Alexandria, were
    married at that place a few days ago. (BMJ, 29 April 1788)

ALLISON, Rev. Dr. Patrick, and Polly, daughter of William Buchanan of Baltimore,
    were married Thursday evening last. (BMJ, 20 March 1787; BMG, 20 March
    1787)

AMOS, James, son of William, and Hannah Lee, daughter of David Lee, were married
    Thursday last at Little Falls Friends Meeting House, Harford Co. (BMJ,
    9 Nov. 1790)

ANDERSON, James, late of Queen Annes Co., deceased; James Hindman, administrator.
    (AMG, 17 April 1788)

ANDERSON, Joseph, died Sunday morning last, merchant of Baltimore, in his 39th
    year. He was a native of Bucks Co., Penna., and prosecuted (sic) business
    in company with Elisha Tyson. His remains were deposited yesterday in the
    Friends Burying Ground in Baltimore. (BMJ, 31 March, 1789)

ANDERSON, Rachel, late of Anne Arundel Co., deceased; Samuel Lane of Calvert Co., executor. (AMG, 5 Nov. 1789)

ANDREWS, Dr. Ephraim, late of Deer Creek, Harford Co., dec.; Peter Hoffman and Cumberland Dugan have been appointed by the "heir to the estate" to settle accounts. (BMG, 10 Oct. 1786 - Extra)

ARNAUD, Peter, French merchant of Baltimore, deceased; creditors should present their claims at the office of the French Consul. (BMG, 17 Oct. 1786; BMJ, 13 Aug. 1786)

ARNOLD, David, late of Calvert Co., dec.; the notice gives a description of the property to be sold. (BMJ, 29 May 1789)

ARNOLD, Mrs. Rebecca, died Wed., 19th inst., at her seat in Lower Marlborough, in her 77th year. (BMJ, 27 Nov. 1788)

ATLEE, Samuel John, a member of the Pennsylvania General Assembly for Lancaster Co., died suddenly at Philadelphia in his 48th year. (BMG, 5 Dec. 1786)

BACKFORD, Miss, died early Tuesday morning, one of the twin daughters of Mr. Wm. Backford of Garrison Forest. She was bitten by a stray dog and died of hydrophobia. (BMJ, 12 June 1789)

BAILLY, Samuel, of Frederick Co., will not pay the debts of his wife Mary. (FMC, 31 May 1786)

BALL, William, married Betsy Dukehart. (BMJ, 29 Oct. 1790)

BANBURY, Mrs., lately from the West Indies, advertises she intends to open a school at her "very cool retired house," the property of John Sellman on Pratt St. (BMJ, 20 July 1790)

BANDELL, Martin, of Baltimore, advertises he intends to leave the state shortly. (BMJ, 31 Jan. 1786)

BANKS, Charles, was a soldier who died in the American army. Nicholas Ridgely Warfield will petition the Assembly of Maryland for relief for the soldier's widow and children. (BMG, 16 April 1790)

BANKSON, Major John, married Saturday evening last, Miss Mickle, daughter of John Mickle of Baltimore, merchant. (BMJ, 8 May 1787)

BARNES, Hannah, late of Anne Arundel Co., deceased; James Barnes of Adam the executor. (BMJ, 7 July 1789)

BARNEY, Mrs. Frances, relict of William Barney, died Friday morning last in her 64th year. Sunday her remains were buried in the family burying ground in Patapsco Neck. (BMJ, 1 July 1788)

BARNEY, Joseph Bosley, late of Baltimore Co., deceased; Rebecca Barney, administratrix. (BMJ, 26 Feb. 1790)

BARRON, Commodore James, died 16th inst., at Hampton, Virginia. (BMJ, 29 May
1787)

BARRY, Capt. John, married Saturday evening last, Mrs. Elizabeth Diffenderfer;
both of Baltimore. (BMJ, 9 March 1790; BMG 12 March 1790)

BARRY, Standish, married Saturday evening last, Nancy Thompson, daughter of
John Thompson of Balto. (BMG, 14 Oct. 1788; BMJ, 14 Oct. 1788)

BARTON, Seth, merchant, married Thursday evening last, Sally Maxwell. (BMJ,
21 Dec. 1790; BMG, 21 Dec. 1790)

BASEY, John, son and heir of John Basey of Balto. Co., dec.; is being sued by
Abraham Larsh, son of Valentine Larsh, dec., concerning a mortgage on a
tract called "Buck's Purchase," 100 a.; the defendant has moved to Virginia.
(AMG, 28 Oct. 1790)

BATE, Charles D., runaway servant of James Hayes, printer, came from Belfast
last summer. (BMG, 6 Jan. 1786)

BATTISTA, John, of Balto., will not pay the debts of his wife Charlotte, who
has eloped from him. (BMG, 20 June 1788)

BAUGHMAN, Christian, died in this town, a very genious industrious architect.
(BMJ, 10 Dec. 1790) George Wehrly, Frederick Haifligh, Elizabeth Baughman acting executors. (BMJ, 10 Dec. 1790)

BAYES, John, from Northamptonshire, Eng., who formerly lived with a farmer in
Patapsco Neck, mear Baltimore, of John's son William, should apply to
Ebenezer Mackie. (BMG, 16 Oct. 1789; BMJ, 9 Oct. 1789)

BAZILL, Ralph, dec.; John Bazill the heir at law, advertises a sale. (AMG,
16 March 1786)

BEARD, Capt. Alexander, married Friday evening last at Fells Point, Polly
Bride. (BMJ, 27 July 1790; BMG, 27 July 1790)

BEATTY, Charles Aphorby, of Georgetown, Potomac, student of medicine, and Miss
Eunice Beal of Philadelphia, were married the 26th ult. (BMG, 3 April 1789)

BECKFORD, Francis Love, lately married in England, Mrs. Lloyd, the widow of
Richard Bennett Lloyd of Md., dec. (BMJ, 27 June 1788)

BELLOC, Francis, planter of Hispaniola, married Sunday evening last, Polly
Barney of Baltimore. (BMJ, 20 Oct. 1789)

3

BENNET, John, of Dor. Co., dec.; owned "New Market," 22 a.; "Bennett's Pasture," 6.a.; "Green Timberyard," 55 a.; "Hog Quarter," 250 a.; Charles Steuart, administrator. (AMG, 30 Dec. 1790)

BERRIDGE, William, of Baltimore, will not pay the debts of his wife Anne. (BMJ, 27 May 1788)

BERRY, Dr. Nicholas, late of Montgomery Co., dec.; Eleanor Berry, executrix. (AMG, 16 Oct. 1788)

BERRY, William, late of Prince Georges Co., dec.; died seized of "Berry's Enclosure," 347 a.; "Oxon Hill," 70 a.; "Holly Spring," 50 a.; William Berry Warman, administrator. (AMG, 1 March 1787)

BEVERIDGE, John, late of Annapolis, deceased; William Coe, administrator. (AMG, 28 Jan. 1790)

BIDDLE, Mrs. Elizabeth, died Saturday last, at Chatsworth, near Baltimore, relict of the late Edward Biddle of Penna., in her 50th year. Her remains were deposited yesterday afternoon in St. Paul's Churchyard. (BMG, 11 Aug. 1789; BMJ, 11 Aug. 1789)

BIDWELL, Thomas, died Thursday last in his 73rd year, formerly a merchant in London. At his request his remains were deposited in the German Baptist Burying Ground. (BMJ, 17 Feb. 1789; BMG, 17 Feb. 1789). James Alcock, executor, will settle the estate. (BMG, 9 Feb. 1790)

BIRD, Empson, late of Cecil Co., deceased; Mary Bird, George Bird, executors. (BMJ, 1 Feb. 1788)

BISCOE, James, Jr., late of St. Marys Co., deceased; John Bond of Thomas, administrator de bonis non. (AMG, 14 Oct. 1790)

BLACKLOCK, Thomas, late of Prince Georges Co., deceased; Nicholas Blacklock, executor. (AMG, 7 Oct. 1790)

BLAKE, ---, age 7, son of Charles Blake, drowned in the Wye River, on 25 July. (BMJ, 10 Aug. 1790) Mr. Blake and his older son, age 15 or 16, were saved. (EMH, 3 Aug. 1790)

BLAKE, Mrs. Sarah, late of Queen Annes Co., deceased; C. T. Wederstrandt, executor. (AMG, 11 March 1790)

BLAKELY, Mrs. Sarah, died yesterday morning, in her 35th year; wife of Josiah Blakely, merchant of Baltimore. (BMJ, 27 March 1787)

BOND, Mrs. Elizabeth, died a few days ago in Middle River Neck, Baltimore Co.; the relict of Capt. William Bond, in her 74th year. (BMJ, 13 Feb. 1787)

BOND, Gerard, late of St. Marys Co., deceased; R'd. Bond, executor. (AMG, 14 Jan. 1790)

BOND, John, son of Joshua, of Fairfax Co., Va., warns his guardians John Dodd and Ann Dodd, not to pay Nichodemus Bond any money arising by virtue of a valuation of lands; John's father is deceased. (BMG, 20 July 1787)

BOND, John, revokes the power of attorney he gave to William Moore, who married Bond's daughter. Bond mentions money due him from the estate of Barney Riley, deceased; also mentions the estate of Col. John Hall, administered by Benedict E. Hall on behalf of his (Bond's?) mother. (BMJ, 23 Sept. 1788)

BOND, Joshua, deceased; three of his tracts about 15 miles from Baltimore are to sold: "Good Luck," 125 a.; "Addition to Good Luck," 25 a.; "Round About Neighbors," 61 a., all adjacent to each other. John Dodd gives notice of the sale. (BMG, 31 March 1786). John Dodd is guardian to John Bond, son of Joshua. (BMJ, 23 June 1786)

BOND, Joshua, late of Baltimore Co., deceased; Samuel Bond, son of Peter, will administer the estate. (BMG, 23 June 1789)

BOND, Nicodemus, of Baltimore Co.; refutes the charges made by John Bond, son of Joshua; mentions his own son Richard Bond. (BMG, 3 Aug. 1787)

BOND, Peter, late of Baltimore Town, conveyed land to John Shewell in 1783, and has since moved from the state. (BMG, 12 June 1787)

BOND, Thomas, died a few days ago, in his 87th year, in Harford Co. He left a widow to whom he had been married for 62 years. (BMJ, 9 May 1788)

BOONE, John, late of Prince George's Co., deceased; Alexius Boone, executor. (AMG, 4 June 1789)

BOOTH, Bartholomew, late of Washington Co., deceased; Alexander Robinson and his wife Priscilla will petition the Assembly for an Act to vest one-half of Booth's real estate in the said Priscilla. (BMJ, 9 Sept. 1788)

BORDLEY, William, Esq., died at his seat in Queen Annes Co., 30th June last, in his 44th year. (BMG, 1 Aug. 1786)

BOURCHETT, Mrs. Maria, wife of John Bourchett, late of Philadelphia, died 27 Nov. 1788. Her remains were interred the following day in the burying ground of the Roman Catholic Chapel. (BMG, 2 Dec. 1788)

BOURCHETTE, Mr., stay-maker from Paris, has moved to the sign of the Indian King in Market Street. (BMG, 28 July 1789)

BOWDOIN, John, of the Eatsern Shore, died in Richmond Co., Va. (BMJ, 18 April 1786)

BOWENE, Joseph Morgan, died Friday last in the prime of life; a native of England. On Saturday evening his remains were deposited in St. Paul's Churchyard. (BMJ, 9 Feb. 1790)

BOWIE, Allen, late of Prince George's Co., deceased; Fielder Bowie, John Fraser Bowie, executors. (AMG, 11 March 1790)

BOYCE, John, Esq., of Harford Co., married Thursday, 19th inst., by Rev. Mr. Wilmer, Miss Rogers, daughter of Benjamin Rogers of Baltimore County. (BMJ, 24 Jan. 1786)

BOYCE, Mr. John, attorney at law, drowned last week when returning to his family in Harford Co., from Baltimore. His body is not yet found. (BMG, 10 Oct. 1786) His body was found Wednesday morning and interred in St. Paul's Churchyard. (BMJ, 13 Oct. 1786) Roger Boyce at Harmony Hall, near Harford Town, will settle the estate. (BMJ, 23 March 1787)

BOYD, Dr. John, died yesterday morning in his 53rd year. (BMJ, 5 Feb. 1790) Ann Boyd and Hercules Courtenay, executors. (BMG, 23 Feb. 1790)

BOYIAN, Mary, of Frederick Co., will petition the Assembly for an act divorcing her from her husband Thomas. (AMG, 5 Aug. 1790)

BRADHURST, Capt. Benjamin, married Sunday 14th inst., Miss Delilah Young. (BMG, 23 March 1790)

BRADLEY, Robert, late of Baltimore, deceased; Ruth Bradley and William Trimble, administrators. (BMG, 20 May 1788)

BRADLEY, Thomas, of Fells Point, died (date not given). (BMJ, 29 April 1788)

BRADSHAW, Joseph, native of St. Marys Co., aged 30 or 31 years, escaped from the Charles Co. jail. (AMG, 9 March 1786)

BRADY, John, died leaving a bequest to the Presbyterian Society near Bladensburg, Prince Georges Co. (AMG, 21 Sept. 1786)

BRASHEAR, Joseph, late of Prince Georges Co., deceased; Alexander Duvall, administrator de bonis non. (AMG, 3 Jan. 1788)

BRAWNER, John Cornish, son and heir at law of Henry Brawner, will petition the next assembly to remedy a defect in a conveyance from Elizabeth Nalley to Barton, Henry, and William Brawner. (AMG, 11 Sept. 1788)

BRENT, Robert, Sr., of Charles Co., deceased; Robert Brent, executor. (AMG, 12 Aug. 1790)

BRERETON, Capt. Thomas, died yesterday morning at an advanced age, a native of Ireland, a nautical commander, insurance broker, and a notary public. (BMJ, 16 Nov. 1787)

BRERETON, Thomas, late of Balto., deceased; Sarah Brereton and James Clark, administrators. (BMJ, 4 Aug. 1789)

BREWER, Henry, late of Anne Arundel Co., deceased; Joseph Brewer, administrator. (AMG, 4 Dec. 1788)

BREWER, John, of Annapolis, deceased; Susanna Brewer, the administratrix, keeps a lodging house in Cornhill Street, Annapolis. (AMG, 21 Aug. 1788)

BREWER, Joseph, late of Anne Arundel Co., deceased; Jane Brewer and Nicholas Brewer, Jr., administrators. (AMG, 18 March 1790)

BRITTON, Samuel, late of Baltimore Co., deceased; Benjamin Gorsuch, administrator. (BMJ, 18 Dec. 1787)

BROADHEAD, Mrs. Rebecca, wife of General Broadhead, lately died at Reading, Penna. (BMJ, 4 March 1788)

BROGDEN, Samuel, deceased; William Brogden, the administrator, advertises a sale. (AMG, 1 March 1787)

BROOKE, Gerard, and Peggy Thomas, daughter of Richard Thomas, were married last Wednesday in Montgomery Co. (BMG, 24 April 1789)

BROOKE, James, late of Montgomery Co., deceased; Samuel Brooke, administrator de bonis non. (BMJ, 16 Feb. 1790) Samuel Brooke advertises a sale of the real estate. (BMJ, 8 June 1790)

BROOKE, Miss Rachel, late of Prince Georges Co., dec.; lived on a tract called "The Vineyard;" Thomas Brooke, administrator. (AMG, 27 Nov. 1788)

BROOKE, Rachel, late of Prince Georges Co., deceased; Clem. Brooke, executor. (AMG 14 Jan. 1790)

BROOKE, Richard, of Montgomery Co., deceased; Roger Brooke, executor. (BMJ, 11 July 1788)

BROOKE, Thomas, of Montgomery Co., dec.; Roger Brooke, executor. (BMJ, 25 Dec. 1789)

BROOKES, Benjamin, of Prince Georges Co., deceased; Sarah Brookes, executrix. (AMG, 8 March 1787)

BROWN, Conrad, of Washington Co., will not pay the debts of his wife Susanna. (EWS, 30 Dec. 1790)

BROWN, Mrs. Frances, died Saturday night last, in her 65th year, relict of Thomas Brown, late of Balto., dec. She was buried yesterday in the Friends Burying Ground. She was eminent in her profession of midwifery. (BMJ, 5 Aug. 1788)

BROWN, Henry, merchant, died Wednesday night last. (BMJ, 21 July 1786) Michael Burke, administrator. (BMJ, 28 July 1786)

BROWN, Henry, late of Baltimore Town, deceased. M. Haslett, administrator. (BMG, 22 Aug. 1788)

BROWN, John, of Dorchester Co., deceased; John Henry, administrator. (AMG, 8 Nov. 1787)

BROWN, Rev. Richard, of Charles Co., died some time ago. (BMJ, 13 Oct. 1789) G. R. Brown, William Brown, and W. B. Magruder, executors. (AMG, 4 Feb. 1790)

BROWNE, Joshua, of Harford Co., deceased; John Thomas Browne, Henry Weatherall, executors. (BMJ, 8 Sept. 1789)

BROWNE, Nathaniel, of Queen Annes Co., deceased; Aquila Browne, Sr., administrator. (BMJ, 28 Aug. 1789)

BROWNING, Benjamin, of Frederick Co., deceased; Jeremiah Browning, executor. (FMC, 22 Nov. 1786)

BRUMFIELD, Francis, of Charles-Town, Cecil Co., will not pay the debts of his wife Elizabeth. (BMJ, 2 Oct. 1787)

BRYAN, John, deceased; Lydia Bryan, Nathan Vennums, executors. (AMG, 23 Sept. 1790)

BRYSON, Catherine, refutes the charges made by her husband. (BMJ, 22 Aug. 1786)

BRYSON, John, of Baltimore, will not pay the debts of his wife Catherine. (BMJ, 11 Aug. 1786)

BUCHANAN, Andrew, died Sunday last at his seat near Baltimore. He was a husband and parent. (BMG, 14 March 1786); He was in his 54th year. (BMJ, 14 March 1786) Sarah Buchanan, George Buchanan of Andrew, and Andrew Buchanan are executors. (BMJ 21 April 1786)

BUCHANAN, Archibald, of Baltimore Co., deceased; Sarah Buchanan the executrix will join others in petitioning the General Assembly for permission to sell the land. The notice gives the names and descriptions of the tracts to be sold. (AMG, 19 July 1787)

BUCHANAN, Dr. George, of Baltimore, married Thursday evening last in Philadelphia, Letitia McKean, second daughter of the Hon. Thomas McKean, Chief Justice of Pennsylvania. (BMJ, 19 June 1789)

BUCHANAN, James, merchant, married Monday evening last, Susannah Young of Phildelphia. (BMJ, 30 Nov, 1787)

BUDD, George, late of Fells Point, deceased; Elizabeth Budd and Amos Loney, executors. (BMJ, 4 Sept. 1787)

BUNTING, William, of Harford Co., deceased; Billy Drew Bunting, executor. (BMJ, 27 Feb. 1787)

BURCH, Anne, of Calvert Co., deceased; B. Burch advertises a sale. (AMG, 19 Jan. 1786)

BURCH, Benjamin, late of Charles Co., deceased; John Winter, creditor, will petition the assembly for a law enabling him to sell as much of the property as he can. (AMG, 2 March 1787)

BURNESTON, Mrs. Anne, died Saturday morning last, in her 64th year, relict of Joseph Burneston, late of Frederick Co. Sunday her remains were deposited in the German Calvinist Churchyard. (BMJ, 26 Oct. 1790)

BURNS, Simon, late of Baltimore, deceased; Hannah Burns administratrix. (BMJ, 21 Sept. 1790) Hannah Birns advertises a sale of all the personal estate of the deceased. (BMJ, 22 Oct. 1790)

BURRELL, Alexander, late of Prince Georges Co., deceased; John Burrell, administrator de bonis non. (AMG, 10 Sept. 1789)

BUSHONG, Philip, late of Washington Co., deceased; Jacob Hess and Christian Newcomer, executors. (BMJ, 20 Jan. 1786)

BUSIGNY, Mr. Victor, died lately in Liverpool in England, a respectable merchant, well known to many gentlemen in this State. (BMJ, 15 April 1788)

CADWAIADER, Gen. John, died 10 Feb. 1786 at Shrewsbury, his seat in Kent Co., in his 44th year. He took an active part in the Revolution. (BMJ, 24 Feb. 1786)

CALDWELL, John, Esq., married Thursday, 16th inst., Miss Caldwell, the daughter of Samuel Caldwell, Esq., of Philadelphia. (BMG, 24 Oct. 1788)

CALLAGHAN, Capt. John, late master of the schooner *Tryal*, deceased; Buchanan and Robb and George Dawson, administrators. (BMJ, 16 Jan. 1787)

CALVERT, Hon. Benedict, died a few days ago at an advanced age at his seat in Prince Georges County. (BMJ, 15 Jan. 1788) Elizabeth Calvert, executrix. (AMG, 17 April 1788)

CAMPBELL, Archibald, merchant, married Thursday last Betsy Hindman. (BMG, 6 June 1786)

CAMPBELL, James, of Baltimore, will not be responsible for the debts of his wife Frances. (BMG, 30 Nov. 1790)

CAMPBELL, John, married last evening Miss Marian Maxwell. (BMJ, 20 May 1788)

CAMPBELL, John, late of Annapolis, deceased; Frances Campbell, executrix. (AMG, 30 Oct. 1788)

CAREY, James, merchant, married Wednesday last, Patty Ellicott, daughter of John Ellicott of Baltimore Co. (BMG, 12 Sept. 1786)

CAREY, Joshua, died lately in Bucks Co., Penna.; merchant of Baltimore. (BMJ, 31 Aug. 1787) Hugh Finlay, administrator. (BMJ, 28 Aug. 1787)

CARLISLE, Dr. John, of the Island of Jamaica, married last evening, Betsy, eldest daughter of of the late Capt. Richard Lane of Baltimore, deceased. (BMJ, 19 Feb. 1790)

CARROLL, Daniel, Jr., late of Montgomery Co., deceased; Notley Young and George Digges, administrators. (AMG, 12 Aug. 1790)

CARROLL, Henry Hill, of Carrollsburg, Charles Co., married a few days ago Mary Rogers, daughter of Benjamin Rogers of Charles Co. (BMJ, 24 Nov. 1789)

CARROLL, James, married Thursday evening, 20th inst., at Perry Hall, Sophia, daughter of Harry Dorsey Gough of Baltimore Co. (BMJ, 25 Dec. 1787)

CARROLL, Martin, advertises his wife Marianna has eloped. (BMJ, 27 June 1786)

CARROLL, Mrs. Rachel, wife of Daniel Carroll, merchant, late a resident of Baltimore Town, died Thursday last in Baltimore Co. On Sunday evening her remains were deposited in St. Paul's Churchyard. (BMJ, 23 Dec. 1788)

CARSEY, Philip, late of Montgomery Co., deceased; Lawrence O'Neale, Alice Carsey, administrators. (AMG, 22 May 1788)

CARSON, Mr. Andrew, merchant of Baltimore, married Thursday evening last, Jane R wland, second daughter of the late William Rowland, Esq., of Cecil Co. (BMG, 18 Aug. 1789)

CARTER, John, of Frederick Co., deceased; Jeremiah Browning, executor. (FMC, 22 Nov. 1786)

CASSEDY, Patrick, was executed near Baltimore Wednesday last. (BMG, 13 Feb. 1789)

CATON, Richard, of Baltimore, married Sunday evening last at Annapolis, Polly, daughter of the Hon. Charles Carroll of Carrollton. (BMJ, 30 Nov. 1787)

CHAMBERLAINE, John, late of Baltimore Co., deceased; Richardson Stuart, administrator. (BMJ, 31 Aug. 1790)

CHAMIER, Mrs., late of Baltimore Co., deceased; Harry D. Gough, John Robert Holliday, Charles R. Carnan, executors. (BMJ, 10 Nov. 1786)

CHAMIER, Daniel, late Sheriff of Baltimore Co.; Harry Dorsey Gough, John Robert Holliday, and Charles R. Carnan advertise they will settle his estate. (BMJ, 16 Feb. 1787)

CHAPLINE, Mrs. Priscilla, wife of James Chapline, and sister of the General Williams of this town, died 27th ult., in Washington Co., in early life. (BMJ, 6 Jan. 1789)

CHAPMAN, Dr. John, late of Charles Co., deceased; Henry H. Chapman will sell the deceased's medicine and books. (AMG, 2 Dec. 1790)

CHARD, Cornelius, late of Anne Arundel Co., deceased; James Moss, executor. (AMG, 20 Sept. 1787)

CHENEY, Dr. Andrew Francis, died 28 Feb. at Princess Anne, Somerset Co., at an advanced age. (BMJ, 23 March 1790)

CHENOWETH, Richard, living on his plantation on Bear Crab Settlement below the Falls in Danville, Ky., had three of his children killed by Indians. His wife was scalped but is expected to recover. Another child was sick in an upper chamber and escaped the massacre. (BMJ, 11 Sept. 1789)

CHENOWETH, Richard, Sr., devised to Richard, Arthur, Thomas, and Joseph Chenoweth the following tracts: "Long Crandon in the Hill," "Henry's Lot," and "Henry's Delight in Amey's Garden;" the properties are to be sold as a result of a suit. (BMJ, 27 July 1790)

CHESELDINE, Mary Neale, died Saturday, 16th inst., at her grandmother's house in St. Marys Co., in her 20th year. (BMJ, 26 Oct. 1790)

CHEW, Phineas, deceased; his land in Cecil Co. to be sold by John Crockett trustee. (BMJ, 24 Aug. 1787)

CLAGGETT, John, died in Montgomery Co., in his 83rd year. (BMJ, 23 Nov. 1790)

CLAPSADLER, George, late of Frederick Co.; has been non compos mentis for over 20 years; owned 150 a. near Pipe Creek. Michael Clapsadler, John Clapsadler, and George Clapsadler, his sons, have sold the land. (BMJ, 10 April 1787)

CLARK, Benjamin, of Anne Arundel Co., will not be responsible for the debts of his wife Rachel. (AMG, 8 Jan. 1789)

CLARK, John, blacksmith of Baltimore Town, married Thursday night last, Ann Mackilvene. (BMG, 11 Dec. 1787)

CLARKE, Joshua, Jr., late of Prince Georges Co., deceased; Anne Clarke administratrix. (AMG, 15 Jan. 1789)

CLAYTON, Solomon; his two year old son was drowned in the River Wye the 25th ult. (EMH, 3 Aug. 1790)

CLOUSE, Mrs. Barbara, died Sunday last in her 55th year, relict of William Clouse. Her remains were interred in the German Calvinist Churchyard. (BMJ, 14 Oct. 1788)

CLOWER, William, of Baltimore, deceased; Charles Schwartz, Nicholas Tschudy, executors. (BMJ, 23 Oct. 1787)

COCKEY, Mrs. Elizabeth, wife of Thomas Deye Cockey, died Wednesday evening last in Baltimore Co. (BMJ, 30 Dec. 1788)

COCKEY, Thomas, late of Balto. Co., dec.; John Cockey of Thomas and Caleb Cockey, execs. (BMJ, 26 June 1789)

COCKEY, Thomas Deye, married Yesterday evening in Balto. Co., Betsy, daughter of John Cockey, Esq. (BMJ, 11 Jan. 1788)

COLE, William, of Harf. Co., dec.; Daniel Scott, administrator. (BMJ, 12 Dec. 1788)

COLLINS, Solomon, wrought in this town some time ago as a mason. His father now lives in Cumberland Co.; he should apply to Tiggat and Hyndman. (BMJ, 14 July 1786)

CONNOWAY, John, late of A. A. Co., dec.; Margaret Connoway, administratrix. (AMG, 17 Dec. 1789)

CONOLLY, John, of Piney Hundred, Fred. Co., will not pay the debts of his wife Honour. (BMJ, 27 March 1789)

CONTEE, Benjamin, Esq., delegate of Maryland to Congress, married a few days ago at Blenheim House, Chas. Co., to Sarah Russell Lee. (BMJ, 8 April 1788)

CONYNGHAM, Capt. John, and Peggy Mathers, daughter of Capt. Joseph Mathers of Fells Point, were married last Tuesday evening. (BMG, 6 Feb. 1787)

COOCH, William, of Newcastle Co., and Peggy Hollingsworth, daughter of Zebulon Hollingsworth, Sr., were married the 24th ult. She was an only daughter. (BMJ, 8 Dec. 1789)

COOK, John, late of Harf. Co., dec.;. William Johnson, exec. (BMG, 14 Dec. 1787)

COOMES, William, late of Chas. Co., dec., bequeathed lands to William Coomes, Sr., Richard Coomes, Clare Thompson, Winnefred Smith, Edward Miles, Elizabeth Smith and Sarah Green. (AMG, 14 Sept. 1786)

COOKE, Ambrose, late of Mont. Co., dec.; William H. Dorsey will settle the estate. (BMJ, 29 Dec. 1789)

COOMES, William, of Chas. Co., married Teresia Clements of the same place, on Tuesday, 27th ult. (BMG, 4 May 1790)

COOPER, John, of Balto., will not pay the debts of his wife Ann who has behaved herself in such a manner that he can no longer live with her, her conduct occasioned by "my malicious neighbours," who have advised her. The next door neighbor to the westward is her principal tutor. (BMJ, 27 June 1786)

COPHER, William, of Washington Co., sold part of "Betsy's Delight," 62 a. and part of "Mistake," 45 a., both in Chas. Co., to Thomas Courtney Reeves; Copher then moved to Kentucky. (AMG, 2 Nov. 1786)

COPPERSMITH, Susanna, widow of George Coppersmith, dec., warns all persons not to take assignments on two bonds passed by her husband to Adam Kesler. (BMJ, 16 May 1788)

CORBLEY, Nicholas, of Balto., married Saturday evening last, Hannah Kneass of Philadelphia. (BMJ, 23 Nov. 1790)

CORMIE, John, a native of Great Britain, master of the grammer school, was killed Sunday, 18th ult., by a fall from his horse. (BMJ, 6 Aug. 1790)

COUCH, Charles, of Balto., and his wife Ann, have parted by mutual consent. (BMJ, 7 July 1786)

COULTER, John, Esq., married at Fells Point Sunday evening last, Polly M'Caskey. (BMJ, 5 Feb. 1788)

COUNSELMAN, Frederick, deceased; Elizabeth Counselman, administratrix. (BMJ, 9 March 1790)

COURTENAY, Mr. Robert, married Betsy, daughter of Richard Burland. (BMJ, 5 Oct. 1790)

COVINGTON, Levin, of P. G. Co., dec.; Susanna Mackall and Levin Mackall, admins. (AMG, 28 Sept. 1786)

COX, Mrs. Jane, late of Balto., Md., died Friday last, in her 50th year. Her remains were interred Saturday in the Friends Burying Ground in this city. "Charleston, S. C., Evening Post, 30th Aug." (BMJ, 14 Sept. 1790)

COX, Mrs. Mary, died Saturday last, relict of brave Capt. James Cox who was killed at the Battle of Germantown. Her remains were interred in the Baptist Churchyard. (BMJ, 26 Feb. 1790) John M'Clellan and James Cox, execs. (BMG, 20 April 1790)

COX, Rebecca, died Wed. morning, 17th inst., aged 17, daughter of Major James Cox, who fell "gloriously fighting for the cause of his country, and the exalted rights of human nature." (BMG, 30 May 1786)

COX, Thomas Smith, late of P. G. Co., dec.; Anne Cox, extx. The notice mentions a deed of trust dated 9 May 1786 from Walter Brooke Cox and wife Anne to Fielder Bowie and Anne Cox. (AMG, 21 Sept. 1786)

COX, William, of Harf. Co., dec.; Mary, John, and William Cox, execs. (BMJ, 15 May 1789)

NEWSPAPER GLEANINGS, 1786 - 1790

CRAWFORD, David, of Frederick Co., dec.; Margaret Crawford and Thomas Sam Pole, administrators. (BMJ, 22 Aug. 1786)

CRESAP, Col. Thomas, dec.; Daniel Cresap, Sr., admin. (FMC, 30 May 1787)

CRISALL, John, late of Annapolis, dec.; John Davidson, Robert Pain Davis, execs. (AMG, 20 April 1786)

CROCKETT, John, merchant of this town, and Miss Graves, daughter of Col. Richard Graves of Kent Co., were married. (BMJ, 28 Nov. 1786)

CROCKETT, John, died Monday last after a lingering illness, late of Baltimore, merchant. His remains were deposited the next day in the Presbyterian Burying Ground. (BMJ, 26 March 1790)

CROMWELL, Mrs., wife of Mr. Cromwell of Fells Point, shipwright, on Tuesday evening last was delivered of three healthy male children. (BMJ, 6 Feb. 1789)

CROMWELL, Nathan, dec.; Jacob Cromwell, administrator. The notice gives a description of the property. (BMJ, 19 Aug. 1788)

CROXALL, Charles, late of Baltimore Co., dec.; James Croxall, exec. (BMJ, 29 May 1789)

CROXALL, James, merchant of Baltimore, married Tuesday evening last, Nelly, daughter of James Gittings, Esq., of Balto. Co. (BMG, 14 March 1788)

CROXALL, Mrs. Rebecca, died Tuesday evening last, in her 58th year; relict of the late Charles Croxall of Baltimore Co. (BMG, 28 Nov. 1786)

CRYDER, Barbara, late of Frederick Co., dec.; Jacob Leamon, exec. (BMG, 12 Dec. 1788)

CUMBRIDGE, Joseph, he and his wife were murdered by savages on 25th of April last, on the head waters of Dunkard Creek, Washington Co., Md. (BMJ, 26 May 1789)

CUNNINGHAM, Capt. Joseph, died Saturday, 5th inst., at the seat of John Smoot of Dor. Co. He was a resident of Boston, New England, where he leaves a wife and daughter. (BMJ, 11 Sept. 1789)

CURRY, William, died 14 Dec. at the house of John Kimmerly, in Shipton-Town, Washington Co. Curry may have had a brother living in some part of Nova Scotia. John Kimmerly will administer the estate. (BMJ, 20 Jan. 1786)

CURSON, Mrs. Elizabeth, died Monday night last, in her 58th year; wife of Richard Curson of Baltimore, merchant. Yesterday her remains were interred in St. Paul's Churchyard. (BMJ, 3 April 1789)

CURSON, Samuel, Esq., of New York, died Monday evening, 24th inst., of a wound received last Friday in a duel with Mr. Burling of Baltimore. "New York, April 26." (BMJ, 2 May 1786)

CURTZ, Jacob, of York Town, Penna., married last Thursday evening, Sukey, daughter of John Schultz of Baltimore. (BMG, 18 Nov. 1788)

DADE, Rose, formerly of King George Co., Va., late of Charles Co., Md., dec.; Gerard B. Causin, exec. (AMG, 2 Feb. 1786)

DALL, James, merchant, married last evening, Charlotte Lane, daughter of the late Capt. Richard Lane, deceased, of Baltimore. (BMJ, 22 Jan. 1790; BMG, 26 Jan. 1790)

DALLAM, Mrs. Frances, died Wednesday, 5th inst., wife of Richard Dallam, Esq., of Abingdon. (BMJ, 14 Sept. 1787)

DALZIELL, Thomas, late of Annapolis, dec.; Margaret Dalziell, extx. (AMG, 30 Dec. 1790)

DARBEY, George, of Montgomery Co., dec.; Basil Darbey, John Darbey, execs. (BMJ, 30 June 1789)

DARNALL, Philip, late of Anne Arundel Co., dec.; devised by his will one moiety of "Addition to St. Jerome's," to Francis Worthey and Mary Worthey. (AMG, 4 Feb. 1790)

DAVENPORT, Capt. Jonathan, of Kent Co., married at Friends' Meeting House, Peggy Duchart of Baltimore. (BMJ, 5 March 1790)

DAVIDGE, Ezekiel, late of Anne Arundel Co., dec.; Rebecca Welch, extx. (AMG, 18 March 1790)

DAVIDGE, Robert, late of Anne Arundel Co., dec.; Joshua Yates, acting exec. (AMG, 11 Sept. 1788)

DAVIDSON, Andrew, late of Baltimore Co., dec.; George Davidson, exec. (BMG, 29 May 1787)

DAVIS, Joseph, of Sassafras River, Cecil Co.;   will not be responsible for the debts of his wife. (BMG, 26 Nov. 1790)

DAVIS, Col. Richard, died 4th inst., at his dwelling on Chew's Farm, Washingon Co., Md., after 12 months illness, in his 63rd year. (BMJ, 12 Oct. 1787)

DAVIS, Robert, Sr., late of Anne Arundel Co., dec.; Ely Davis, Ichabod Davis, administrator. (BMJ, 12 Jan. 1790)

DAVIS, William, Sr., of Fells Point, Baltimore; Stephen Wilson, Robert Lemmon, trustees. (BMG, 9 Oct. 1787)

DAVIS, William, of Anne Arundel Co., dec.; Allen Quynn, admin. (AMG, 2 Oct. 1789)

DAVIS, William, Jr., of Anne Arundel Co., dec.; Allen Quynn, administrator. (AMG, 21 Jan. 1790)

DAY, Mrs. Mary Gouldsmith, consort of Capt. John Day, of Harford Co., died 18th Sept. last, in her 29th year. She leaves a husband and numerous offspring. (BMJ, 17 Oct. 1786)

DEALE, Thomas, of near Herring Creek, dec.; Thomas Pownall and wife and Joseph Deale,execs. (AMG, 2 Feb. 1786) Deale owned a plantation near Herring Creek Church. Joseph Deale the only exec. (AMG, 1 Jan. 1789; AMG, 30 Dec. 1790)

DEANS, Christian, late of Baltimore Co., dec.; Waltara Bowman, extx. (BMJ, 17 Nov. 1786)

DEAVER, John, dec.; John Deaver, the exec., will sell "Parker's Folly," in Harford Co., between Bush River and Rumney Creek, which had been patented to John Parker, and sold by Parker's son, John, to Henry Rhodes, and sold by Rhodes' son George Lester Rhodes, to the deceased. (BMJ, 24 Feb. 1786)

DE BEAUPRE, Charles Dupuid, died Tuesday evening last, in his 98th year. He was one of the neutral French brought to this town in 1755, and was a native of Annapolis Royal in Nova Scotia. (BMG, 17 Dec. 1790: the name is given as Charles Dupuy in BMJ, 17 Dec. 1790)

DE CORSE, Capt. John, was murdered. One Davenport has been arrested for the crime, and lodged in Talbot Co., jail. (BMJ, 3 June 1788)

DE GRASSE, Count, died in Paris, 13th Jan. He was taken prisoner by Admiral Rodney in the West Indies, after a bloody conflict which lasted from six in the morning to the same hour in the evening. (BMJ, 15 April 1788)

DE LA ROCHE, Gilbert, dec.; Christopher Johnston, Thomas Usher, Jr., trustees. (BMJ, 9 May 1786)

DENT, George, late of Charles Co., dec.; Eleanor Dent, Henry Dent, George Dent, execs. (AMG, 26 Jan. 1786)

DENT, Peter, late tobacco inspector, Charles Co., dec.; Anne Dent and Theodore Dent, admins. (AMG, 27 March 1788)

NEWSPAPER GLEANINGS, 1786 - 1790

DENT, Capt. Thomas, dec.; Elizabeth Dent, administratrix. (AMG, 10 Sept. 1789)

DE PLASNE, John Claudius Joseph Gagneur, native of Poligny, France, former
    officer in the Light Horse of that Kingdom, died Saturday evening last in
    Baltimore, in his 36th year. (BMJ, 20 April 1790)

DESHER, John, late of Old Town, Baltimore, dec.; Mary Desher, extx.

DEVILBISS, Mrs. Barbara, consort of George Devilbiss of Baltimore, merchant,
    died Wednesday morning last, aged 32 years. Her remains were interred in
    the Reformed German Churchyard. (BMJ, 6 Nov. 1789)

DE WITT, Mrs. Elizabeth, wife of Thomas De Witt, died Monday last. Her remains
    were deposited in the Presbyterian Churchyard. (BMJ, 27 Jan. 1786)

DICK, James, merchant of Annapolis, dec.; Mary M'Culloch, C. Steuart, and J.
    McCulloch, execs. (AMG, 30 Dec. 1790)

DICKINSON, James, of Tal. Co., dec.; John Singleton, exec.; the notice gives a
    description of the deceased's farm. (BMJ, 22 April 1788)

DIGGES, Ignatius, of Mellwood Park, Prince Georges Co., dec.; Mary Digges will
    settle the estate. (AMG, 23 Feb. 1786)

DONNELLY, Peter, on Wednesday last, with Peter Mooney, was executed for
    assaulting and robbing David Stoddard of Baltimore Town on 31st December
    last. (BMJ, 21 March 1788)

DORSEY, Edward, Esq., of Elk Ridge, married Saturday last, Betsey Dorsey, the
    eldest daughter of Col. John Dorsey of Baltimore. (BMG, 28 March 1786)

DORSEY, Harry Woodward, married Polly, daughter of Zachariah Maccubbin of
    Baltimore Co. (BMJ, 28 Feb. 1786)

DORSEY, John Crockett, dec.; Elizabeth Dorsey, extx.; Benjamin Musgrove warns
    all persons from receiving from her an assignment of his note. (FMC, 7
    June 1786; FMC, 13 Sept. 1786)

DORSEY, Joshua, Sr., late of Anne Arundel Co., dec.; Philemon Dorsey and Benja-
    min Dorsey, execs. (BMJ, 1 June 1790)

DORSEY, Nicholas, Jr., of Anne Arundel Co., was killed Tuesday evening last
    when his horse stumbled and he was thrown against the stump of a small
    tree. (BMJ, 10 Oct. 1788)

DORSEY, Nicholas, son of Henry, dec.; resided at Elk Ridge, Anne Arundel Co.;
    Lucy Dorsey, administratrix. (AMG, 29 Jan. 1789)

DORSEY, Samuel, son of John, dec.; Ely Dorsey, exec. (BMJ, 9 June 1786)

DORSEY, William, married Tuesday, 2nd inst., at Fair Hill, Montgomery Co.,
    Miss Brooke, daughter of Richard Brooke, late of that county. (BMJ, 19
    March 1790)

DOVE, William, late of Anne Arundel Co., dec.; Sarah Dove, admnx. (AMG, 8
    July 1790)

DOYLE, John, runaway Irish servant man of Samuel Turner of Prince Georges Co.;
    Doyle may have a relative living in Baltimore. (BMG, 28 Feb. 1786)

DOYLE, Michael, dec.; William M'Quinn, admin. (BMG, 24 April 1789)

DOYNE, Jesse, late of Charles Co., dec.; Anne Doyne, extx. (AMG, 2 March 1786)

DRANE, James, late of Prince Georges Co., dec.; Elizabeth Drane and James Drane
    execs. (AMG, 26 Nov. 1789)

DUBIAIN, John, died last Saturday morning at a villa near Baltimore; from Cape
    Francois; being in a state of insanity, he shot himself through the head
    with a musket. (BMJ, 2 June 1789)

DUGAN, Cumberland, merchant, married Tuesday evening last, Peggy, eldest daughter
    of James Kelson of Baltimore. (BMG, 7 Nov. 1786)

DULANY, Elizabeth, wife of Walter Dulany, will petition the Assembly for resti-
    tution of certain confiscated property of her former husband, Lloyd Dulany.
    (AMG, 1 Nov. 1787)

DUNBAR, William, born in Portfoy, Banffshire, North Britain, came to America
    about four years ago. (AMG, 13 April 1786)

DUVALL, Mrs. Mary, died Wednesday evening last at Annapolis, in her 29th year;
    consort of Gabriel Duvall. (BMJ, 30 March 1790)

EAGLESTONE, Abraham, late of Baltimore Co., dec.; Jonathan Eaglestone and
    Vincent Green, execs. (BMJ, 7 March 1786)

EASTBURN, Benjamin, late of George-Town, dec.; Jane Eastburn and Robinson
    Eastburn, admins. (BMG, 6 Nov. 1787)

EASTMAN, Joseph, late of Annapolis, dec.; James Williams, admin. (AMG, 5
    April 1787)

EATON, Mr., a householder, drowned Sunday week last, when crossing from Kent
    Island to Annapolis. (EMH, 14 Sept. 1790)

EATON, John, hatter, of Baltimore, died Sunday morning last in his 31st year. (BMJ, 24 Feb. 1789) Samuel Grey, exec. (BMJ, 24 March 1789)

ECKSTEIN, Dr. Gideon, died at Ephrata, seat of the mother church of the Dunkards, on 26th ult., in his 70th year. (FMC, 22 Aug. 1787)

EDELEN, Christopher, died Saturday morning last at an advanced age. His remains were interred in the Roman Catholic burial ground. (FMC, 1 Feb. 1786) M. Bayly, admin. (FMC, 8 March 1786)

EDEN, Capt. John, late of St. Marys Co., dec.; Margaret Eden, extx. (AMG, 1 May 1788) Charles Llewellin also an exec. (AMG, 25 Sept. 1788)

EDEN, John, Sr., late of St. Marys Co., dec.; Walter Stone of Charles Co., admin. de bonis non. (BMJ, 14 April 1789)

EDEN, Townshend, late of St. Marys Co., dec.; Betty Anne Eden, Walter Stone, admins. (AMG, 10 Jan. 1788)

EDWARDS, Aquila, late of Anne Arundel Co., dec.; William Edwards, admin. (AMG, 25 March 1790)

EDWARDS, Edward, late of Anne Arundel Co., dec.; Anne Edwards, Aquila Edwards, William Edwards, Cadwalader Edwards, Jonathan Edwards, execs. (AMG, 6 July 1786)

EDWARDS, Paul, of Baltimore, will not pay the debts of his wife Sarah. (BMJ, 10 Feb. 1786)

ELDER, Ely, late of Anne Arundel Co., dec.; owned part of "Taylor's Park;" Elizabeth Elder, admnx (AMG, 11 March 1790)

ELDER, Owen, of Baltimore Co., dec.; Charles Dorsey of Nicholas was appointed a trustee by the Chancery Court to dispose of Elder's real estate. (BMJ, 2 Feb. 1790)

ELLIOTT, James, of Harford Co., dec.; Agness Elliott, extx. (BMJ, 2 June 1789)

ELLIOTT, Thomas, dec.; James Elliott, heir at law; Catherine Elliott and David Steuart, admins. (AMG, 16 Aug. 1787)

EVANS, Joseph, merchant, married last evening, Eliza Davey of Baltimore. (BMG, 4 Dec. 1789)

EVERSFIELD, John, late of Prince Georges Co., dec.; Barbara Eversfield, admnx. (AMG, 20 April 1786)

EWING, Patrick, late of Dorchester Co., dec.; Robert Ewing, exec. (EMH, 14 Dec. 1790)

FAUNTLEROY, Mr. Griffin, of Kent Island, Queen Annes Co., dec.; Dekar Thompson, admin. (AMG, 24 Sept. 1789)

FAW, Mrs. Juliana, wife of Abraham Faw, Esq., of Frederick Town, died Friday, 15th inst., in her 48th year. (BMJ, 22 Aug. 1788)

FALLS, Mrs. Abigail, wife of Dr. Moore Falls of Petersburgh, Va., and daughter of the Hon. Edward Biddle, late of Penna., dec.; died Tuesday last at Chatsworth, seat of George Lux, Esq., near Baltimore, in her 23rd year. She was interred in St. Paul's Church. (BMJ, 16 Jan. 1789)

FELL, William, died Friday night last, in his 27th year, late Proprietor of Fells Point. (BMJ, 10 Oct. 1786)

FELL, William, late of Baltimore, dec.; Thomas Bond warns the tenants of the late Fell not to pay any rents to Edward Fell Day. (BMJ, 15 Sept. 1789)

FENDALL, Mrs., died in Baltimore, consort of Philip Richard Fendall, Esq., of Alexandria. (BMJ, 19 May 1789)

FENDALL, Benjamin, late of Charles Co., dec.; Mary Trueman Fendall, admnx. (AMG, 24 Aug. 1786)

FENESEY, John, son of William, should get in touch with his father, who is anxious to hear from him. A letter directed to the care of Samuel Cleland at Big Pipe Creek Bridge, Frederick Co., will be forwarded. (FMC, 30 Aug. 1786)

FENWICK, Enoch, late of St. Marys Co., dec.; Joseph Millard, exec. (AMG, 2 Aug. 1787)

FERNANDES, Abraham Lopes, late of Baltimore, dec.; George Salmon, admin. (BMJ, 23 Nov. 1787)

FISHER, Dr. Adam, died Thursday last at the age of 51, a respectable citizen of Frederick. (FMC, 22 Aug. 1787) Margaret Fisher, extx. (AMG, 3 Sept. 1789)

FISHER, John, brushmaker from Lancaster, now carries on the brushmaking business in Baltimore. (AMG, 7 Jan. 1790)

FITE, Henry, of Baltimore Town, deceased; Henry Fite and George Reinecker, execs. (BMG, 27 Nov. 1789)

FITZGERALD, James, of Baltimore Co., dec.; Jane Fitzgerald, extx. (BMJ, 21 March 1786)

FLOYD, James, will not pay the debts of his wife Eleanor, who has eloped from him; resides in Baltimore. (BMJ, 25 May 1790)

NEWSPAPER GLEANINGS, 1786 - 1790

FORD, John, son of William, of Baltimore Co., intends to petition the Assembly
    (to confirm?) his right to part of a tract called "Benjamin's Beginning
    and Benjamin's Addition." (BMG, 17 Nov. 1789)

FORMAN, William, of Chester-Town, Kent Co., married Saturday evening last,
    Jane, daughter of the late William Spear. (BMJ, 23 Nov. 1790)

FORREST, Sarah, of Anne Arundel Co., defends herself against the charges of
    her husband. They have been married for five years and have four children.
    (BMJ, 26 Sept. 1786)

FORREST, John, of Anne Arundel Co., will not pay the debts of his wife Sarah,
    who has left his bed and board. (BMJ, 8 Sept. 1786)

FORREST, Col. Uriah, married Sunday evening, 11th inst., at Sotterley Hall,
    St. Marys Co., Rebecca, daughter of the Hon. George Plater. (BMJ, 23
    Oct. 1789)

FORSTER, Ralph, of Anne Arundel Co., dec.; George Digges, admin. (AMG, 12 March
    1789) Forster lived on "Hill's Delight." (AMG, 12 Nov. 1789)

FORSYTH, Capt. Robert, late of Fells Point, dec.; James Tibbitt and Sarah Tibbitt,
    admnx. (BMG, 26 Oct. 1787)

FOSTER, William, of Baltimore, will not pay the debts of his wife Sarah. (BMG,
    28 Oct. 1788)

FOWLE, John, (of Baltimore), dec.; Englehard Yeiser and Peter Frick, execs.
    (BMJ, 16 March 1787)

FOWLER, Thomas, late of Anne Arundel Co., dec.; Vachel Gaither, T. Bicknell,
    admins. de bonis non. (AMG, 10 Dec. 1789)

FOWLER, Walter, of Queen's St., Fells Point, will not pay the debts of his
    wife Margaret, who eloped from him on 22nd inst. (BMJ, 24 Aug. 1787)

FRAIZER, Alexander, dec.; John Alex. Fraizer, admin. (AMG, 21 Oct. 1790)

FRANKLIN, Benjamin, patriot, philosopher, and citizen, died Saturday night
    last in Philadelphia, in his 85th year. (BMJ, 23 April 1790)

FRANKLIN, John, of West River, dec.; W. Murray, admin. de bonis non. (AMG,
    17 D c. 1789)

FRANKLIN, Thomas, late of Balto. Co., dec.; James Franklin, admin. (BMJ, 3
    July 1787)

FRAZIER, William, late of Anne Arundel Co., dec.; John Frazier, admin. (AMG,
    Dec. 1789)

FREELAND, Francis, late of Prince Georges Co., dec.; Mary Freeland, Francis Freeland, and Martha Sampson, execs. (BMJ, 21 Feb. 1786)

GAITHER, Col. Edward, died Monday, 24th inst., at the Woodyard, the seat of Stephen West, in Prince Georges Co. (BMJ, 2 Oct. 1787)

GAITHER, Edward, son of Edward, advertises sale of 400 acres, part of his dwelling plantation, called "Gaither's Collection." (BMJ, 13 Nov. 1789)

GAITHER, Evan, of Elk Ridge, offers for sale 5000 acres of land on the north side of Kentucky River in Fayette Co., Ky. (BMJ, 13 April 1790)

GALLAGAR, Charles, of Baltimore, will not pay the debts of his wife. (BMJ, 20 May 1788)

GANTT, Dr. Edward, of Prince Georges Co., intends to move to Va. early in the spring. Jonathan Simmons will settle his debts. (AMG, 12 Jan. 1786)

GARTRELL, Richard, of Frederick Co., dec.; Charles Gartrell, admin. (FMC, 18 Jan. 1786)

GARTS, Mrs. Margaret, died in Fredericksburg, Va., wife of Peter Garts, late of this town. (BMJ, 10 Nov. 1789)

GARTS, Peter, son of Charles Garts, merchant of Baltimore, married 25th ult. at Fredericksburg, Va., Peggy, daughter of Robert Lilly, merchant of Fredericksburg. (BMG, 5 Dec. 1788)

GARY, Gideon, dec.; Elizabeth Gary, Leonard Sellman, execs. (AMG, 11 May 1786)

GASSAWAY, Thomas, dec.; Eliza Gassaway, admnx. (AMG, 23 Sept. 1790)

GATES, Major General Horatio, married Monday last in Washington Co., Mary Vallance. (BMJ, 4 Aug. 1786)

GAY, Mrs. Anne, died Sunday evening at the house of William Russell, Esq., of this county; daughter of the late Darby Lux, and widow of the late Nicholas Ruxton Gay. (BMJ, 11 July 1786)

GEDDES, David, intends to remove from Annapolis, and is anxious to settle his affairs. (AMG, 8 April 1790)

GEORGE, Joshua, married this day at Cecil, Betsy, fourth daughter of the Rev. Mr. Thompson. "Cecil- 21 Dec. 1786." (BMJ, 26 Dec. 1786)

GEROCH, Mrs., wife of Rev. George Siegfried Geroch, minister of the German Lutheran Congregation in Baltimore, died Wednesday last. (BMJ, 27 April 1787)

GEROCK, Mr. George Sigfried, died Saturday night last, in his 66th year; Pastor of the German Lutheran Church in Baltimore. (BMJ, 28 Oct. 1788; longer notice in BMJ, 31 Oct. 1788). His name is given as John Sigfried Gerock in BMG, 28 Oct. 1788.

GEROCK, Samuel, merchant, married Tuesday evening last, by Rev. Dr. Cutting, Sarah Wallce. "Newbern, ' N. C., 27 Dec." (BMJ, 1 Feb. 1788)

GERRY, John, Esq., died in Marblehead. (BMJ, 10 Feb. 1786)

GIBSON, Jacob, late of Talbot Co., dec.; David Kerr, admin. (EMH, 11 May 1790)

GILDER, Dr. Reuben, married Tuesday evening last, Polly Alkins. (BMJ, 8 Oct. 1790)

GILES, Mrs. Ann, died Saturday last, the amiable consort of James Giles, Esq., and mother of William Fell, Esq., Proprietor of Fells Point. (BMJ, 14 April 1786)

GILES, Jacob, Sr., of Harford Co., dec.; Thomas Giles, and P. Coale, execs.; the notice gives a description of the property. (BMJ, 9 Dec. 1788)

GILLELEN, Peter, near Taneytown, will be responsible for the debts of his wife Margaret. (BMJ, 19 May 1786)

GILLINGHAM, John, of the Forks of the Gunpowder, Baltimore Co., will not pay the debts of his wife Sarah. (BMJ, 29 Aug. 1786)

GILPIN, Joseph, died Tuesday last, after a short illness, at his seat near Elkton, Cecil Co. (BMJ, 2 April 1790)

GIST, Miss Nancy, died Thursday last on Kent Island, where she was visiting; the daughter of Joshua Gist of Frederick Co., Md. (BMJ, 3 Sept. 1790)

GITTINGS, Richard, merchant, married last evening, Polly, eldest daughter of the late John Sterrett, Esq. (BMJ, 21 Nov. 1788)

GODDARD, Elias Kingston, died Wednesday evening last in his 22nd year; a native of Mass., who arrived a few days ago from Jamaica. (BMJ, 14 Nov. 1788)

GODDARD, William, printer of Baltimore, married at Cranston, by the Rev. Mr. Oliver, Miss Abigail Angell, daughter of the late Brigadier General Angell, on Thursday last. "Providence - 27 May." (FMC, 28 June 1786)

GODMAN, Richard, aged 21, died lately of smallpox at Stockholm, near Elk Ridge Landing, brother of Capt. Samuel Godman. (BMG, 15 Jan. 1788)

GOLD, Oliver, mariner, late of Baltimore Co., dec.; Martha Gold and Cyprian Wells, admins. (BMG, 19 Feb. 1788)

GOLDSBOROUGH, Nicholas, of Talbot Co., died 6th inst., in his 28th year. He had been bitten by a mad dog. He leaves a wife and an infant son. (BMJ, 23 May 1788)

GOLDSBOROUGH, Robert, died at Cambridge, 31st ult.,...distinguished patriot and Attorney General of Maryland (long obit is given). (AMG, 5 Jan. 1789; BMJ, 16 Jan. 1789)

GOLDSBOROUGH, Robert, Jr., of Cambridge, drowned Sunday, 5th inst., as he was crossing the bay from Kent Island to Annapolis. He was in his 24th year. (BMG, 14 Sept. 1790)

GOLDSBOROUGH, Mrs. Sarah, wife of Robert Goldsborough, Esq., of Dor. Co., died Tuesday morning last in Talbot Co. (BMJ, 8 May 1787)

GOODMAN, Joseph, came to reside in Maryland many years ago from Peterborough, England. He should apply to Evan Thomas of Montgomery Co. or to Elias Ellicott of Baltimore. (BMJ, 10 March 1789)

GORDON, Rev. John, died Sunday, 7th inst., in his 77th year, at his dwelling house, Rector of St. Michael's Parish for more than 40 years. (BMJ, 16 March 1790)

GOTT, Ezekiel, late of Anne Arundel Co., dec.; Ezekiel Gott, exec.; (AMG, 19 Feb. 1789)

GOTT, Walter, and Mrs. Anne Gott, both of Anne Arundel Co., dec.; Benjamin Burgess and John Chew, administrators de bonis non. (AMG, 6 Nov. 1788)

GOULD, Oliver, of Baltimore, dec.; Martha Goulding (sic) and Cyprian Wells, execs. (BMJ, 16 Oct. 1789). See Oliver Gold, above.

GRAHAM, John, of Calvert Co., married at Frederick Co., Miss Johnson, daughter of the Hon. Thomas Johnson, Esq. (BMJ, 29 Jan. 1788)

GRANT, Alexander, cooper, drowned Thursday evening last, as a result of rains and flooding of Jones Falls. (BMJ, 10 Oct. 1786). Mary Grant, admnx. (BMJ, 15 June 1787)

GRANT, Mrs. Elizabeth Ruth, died Monday evening last, in her 49th year, wife of Daniel Grant of Baltimore. Her remains were interred in St. Pauls Church yard. (BMJ, 25 Sept. 1789)

GRANTHAM, Jacob, died Tuesday night last, aged 53 years; of Baltimore. (BMG, 16 Nov. 1787)

GRAY, Adam, of Queen Annes Co., dec.; W. Hayward, admin. (EMH, 16 Nov. 1790)

GRAY, John Nelson, resided near Ellicotts Lower Mill, dec.; Susannah Gray, admnx. (BMG, 23 Nov. 1787)

GRAY, Samuel, and Miss Nancy Rice, both of Baltimore, were married Saturday evening last. (BMG, 25 Sept. 1787)

GRAY, Zachariah, dec.; Sophia Gray, extx. (AMG, 18 May 1786)

GRAYSON, Col. William, U. S. Senator, died Friday, 12th inst., on his way to Congress. (BMJ, 19 March 1790)

GREEN, John, (of Annapolis?), dec.; George Davis, admin. (AMG, 22 Oct. 1789)

GREEN, Richard, of Anne Arundel Manor, Prince George's Co., dec.; Jacob Green, brother of dec., admin. (AMG, 18 June 1789)

GREENE, Nathaniel, died Monday, 19th June last, at his seat near Savannah, Ga., late Major General in the U. S. Army. (FMC, 19 July 1786)

GREENHOW, John, of Williamsburg, Va., in his 64th year, merchant, was lately married to Miss Harman, aged about 16, of James City. (BMG, 28 March 1786)

GREENWAY, John, lived in Liverpool, Eng., and left that town about 35 years ago to reside in Maryland. He should apply to the printer. (BMJ, 10 Jan. 1786)

GRIFFIN, Thomas, late of Anne Arundel Co., dec.; Thomas Griffin, admin. (BMG, 13 April 1790)

GRIFFIN, Thomas, late of Anne Arundel Co., dec.; Thomas Griffin, Jr., admin. (AMG, 27 May 1790)

GRIFFITH, Mrs. Elizabeth, wife of Nathan Griffith, died yesterday morning. (BMG, 6 July 1790)

GRIFFITH, Joshua, late of Anne Arundel Co., dec.; Dennis Griffith, surviving exec. (AMG, 16 April 1789)

GRIFFITH, Sally, died Saturday evening, of Baltimore, aged 16 years. Her remains were interred next to her parents in the Baptist Churchyard. (BMJ, 19 Aug. 1788)

GRIST, Dr. George, died Saturday late; only son of Isaac Grist, Esq., coroner, of Fells Point. (BMG, 12 Sept. 1786)

GROMETH, Jacob, of Frederick Co., dec.; Michael Bayer, admin. (FMC, 7 Nov. 1787)

GROOMBRIDGE, James, native of England who lived for some time at or near Slade's Tavern or My Lady's Manor, and kept a school, should apply to Wallace and Muir of Annapolis. (BMJ, 12 Jan. 1787)

GROSJEAN, J. J., merchant, married Polly Trickle. (BMJ, 29 Oct. 1790)

GUTTRY, Mrs. Susannah, wife of Joshua Guttry, and youngest daughter of Melcher Keener, merchant, died Thursday last. On Saturday her remains were deposited in the German Calvinist Churchyard. (BMJ, 27 Jan. 1789)

GWINN, Mrs. Anne, late of Charles Co., dec.; Thomas Claggett of Piscattaway and Edward Gwinn will settle the estate. (AMG, 11 June 1789)

GWINN, Mrs. Jane, wife of John Gwinn, died at Taneytown on 7th inst., in her 32nd year. (BMJ, 17 April 1789)

HACKET, John, merchant, married Tuesday evening last, Jenny, daughter of Daniel Grant of this town. (BMJ, 4 Jan. 1788)

HAGER, Francis, late of Baltimore, dec.; Robinson Jones, Margaret Hager, admins. (BMJ, 14 Sept. 1790)

HALL, Edward, late of Frederick Co., dec.; William Hall and Marsh M. Duvall, execs. (AMG, 5 Jan. 1786)

HALL, Edward, son of Henry, late of Anne Arundel Co., dec.; Martha Hall, admnx. (AMG, 4 May 1786)

HALL, Edward, late of Harford Co., dec.; Josias Hall, exec. (BMJ, 5 Sept. 1788)

HALL, Mrs. Elizabeth, late of Anne Arundel Co., dec.; Henry Hall, Joseph Howard, execs. (AMG, 12 Feb. 1789)

HALL, Francis, late of Prince Georges Co., dec.; Benjamin Hall, exec. (AMG, 18 Sept. 1788)

HALL, John, of Cecil Co., will not pay the debts of his wife Ann. (BMJ, 21 Nov. 1786)

HALL, John, late of West River, Anne Arundel Co., dec.; William Henry Hall, exec. (AMG, 19 Aug. 1790)

HALL, Thomas Henry, Esq., of Washington Co., died 7th inst., as a result of a fall from a horse. (BMJ, 14 Nov. 1788). Barbara Hall, extx. (AMG, 2 July 1789)

HAMERSLEY, William, of St. Marys Co., dec.; F. Hamersley and Henry Hamersley, exec. (AMG, 16 Dec. 1790)

HAMILTON, James, will not pay the debts of his wife Elizabeth. (BMG, 16 June 1789)

HAMILTON, Ralph, late of Fells Point, dec.; Hamilton, James, admin. (BMG, 18 April 1788)

HAMMOND, Ann, late of Anne Arundel Co., dec.; Hamutel Welsh will settle the estate. (BMG, 20 Feb. 1787)

HAMMOND, Mrs. Elizabeth, died Tuesday last, consort of John Hammond, of Baltimore, merchant. (BMJ, 25 April 1788)

HAMMOND, James, of Charlestown, Va., married at Berkeley Co., Va., Polly Rankin, only daughter of R. Rankin of Berkeley. (BMJ, 5 Feb. 1789)

HAMMOND, Mr. Matthias, late of Anne Arundel Co., dec.; Philip Hammond, exec. (AMG, 17 May 1787)

HAMMOND, Mrs. Rachel, died Tuesday morning last (11 April), relict of Philip Hammond, in her 75th year. (AMG, 13 April 1786)

HAMMOND, Thomas, has deeded all his property to his brother William Hammond. (AMG, 10 April 1788)

HAMMOND, Thomas H., died Monday last, in his 21st year; son of the late Capt. Hammond. (BMJ, 5 Nov. 1790)

HANNA, Grizelda, will petition the General Assembly for an act allowing her to divorce her present husband. (BMG, 9 Sept. 1788)

HANNA, Rev. William, late of Anne Arundel Co., dec.; Serah Hanna, admnx. (AMG, 9 Nov. 1786)

HANNAM, Minty, left England about 1768, and was heard of at Christopher Cardiff's, Great Choptank River, Bolingbroke, Talbot Co., in 1771. He should apply to Rev. Reader Wareham, Dorchester, Eng. Anyone knowing of his death should apply to Messrs. John and Thomas Gilliats of Richmond, Va. (BMJ, 13 March 1789)

HANNAN, Patrick, late of Fells Point, dec.; Elizabeth Hannan and John Hannan, execs. (BMJ, 24 Feb. 1789)

HANSON, Amon, late of Baltimore Co., dec.; Josias Pennington, Wm. Askew, and Jonathan Rutter, admins. (BMJ, 2 May 1786)

HANSON, Edward, late of Baltimore Co., dec.; Josias Pennington, Wm. Askew, and Jonathan Rutter, admins. (BMJ, 2 May 1786)

HANSON, Mr. Jonathan, died Friday night last, at his seat near this town. (BMJ, 3 Jan. 1786) Henry Stevenson, Solomon Hillen, execs. (BMJ, 7 July 1786)

HARNETT, John Maurice, a native of Ireland, and a tanner by trade, came to this town last November in the Brig Baltimore from Cork. He should apply to the printer. (BMJ, 13 Aug. 1790)

HARREY, Martin, late of Hagerstown, Washington Co., dec.; Jonathan Harrey and David Harrey, execs. (BMJ, 7 April 1789)

HARRIS, Arthur, late of Calvert Co., dec.; Benj. Harris, III, exec. (AMG, 28 May 1789)

HARRIS, Benton, late of Worcester Co., dec.; John Purkins, Rebecca Costen, John Smith, John Hayman, and John Riggen will petition the Assembly for an act to appoint a trustee to sell the lands of the deceased. (AMG, 15 Oct. 1789)

HARRIS, Benton, deceased; formerly lived in Worcester Co., near Snow Hill. He devised his lands to John Rousby Whittington, with the understanding that if the said Whittington died without heirs, and Harris' widow also died, the lands were to be sold. (EMH, 23 Nov. 1790)

HARRIS, David, merchant, married Wednesday evening last, Mrs. Frances Moale, relict of the late Richard Moale of Baltimore. (BMG, 29 Jan. 1788)

HARRISON, Mr. John, of Frederick Co., dec.; Joseph Sim and Thomas Gantt advertise a sale of his property including 452 acres of "Addison's Choice," which the deceased purchased of the State of Maryland. (FMC, 16 May 1787)

HARRISON, Dr. Joseph, died yesterday morning at Fells Point, aged 38 years. Funeral will be held from the house of the widow Dawson. (BMJ, 20 April 1790) William Chester, admin. (BMJ, 7 May 1790)

HARRISON, Robert Hanson, died 2 April 1790 at his seat on Patowmack River in Charles Co., in his 45th year; Chief Judge of the General Court of Maryland. (BMJ, 13 April 1790) Walter Harrison, admin. (BMJ, 18 June 1790)

HARRISON, Hon. William, died Tuesday, 21st ult., at his residence in Charles Co., a member of the Senate of Maryland. (BMG, 18 Aug. 1789)

HARRY, Martin, dec.; Susanna Harry and Jacob Harry, admins. (EWS, 18 Nov. 1790)

HARWOOD, Mr. William, died 16th August at King and Queen Court House in his 31st year. (BMG, 8 Sept. 1789)

HASLET, Samuel, late of Baltimore Town, dec.; Thomas B. Usher, Joseph Donaldson, Samuel Johnston, Joseph Usher, execs. of Thomas Usher. (BMG, 15 Aug. 1786)

HATTON, Thomas, of Baltimore Co., will not pay the debts of his wife Mary. (BMJ, 17 Oct. 1786)

HAUN, Michael, late of Baltimore Co., dec.; David Kephart, Jacob Haun, execs.; they advertise the sale of part of "Frankfort," six miles below Westminster, now occupied by Adam Haun. (BMJ, 6 Feb. 1787)

HAWKINS, George Frazier, late of Prince Georges Co., dec.; Susanna T. Hawkins, extx. (AMG, 19 Jan. 1786)

HAWKINS, Col. Josias, died 30 October last, at his seat in Charles Co., in his 54th year, leaving a widow and children. (BMJ, 17 Nov. 1789)

HAY, John, late of the Island of Tobacco (sic), dec.; Nehemiah Sangster of Harford Co., deceased's executor. (BMG, 27 Oct. 1789)

HAYES, James, died Friday last, in his 84th year, formerly a citizen of Liverpool in England. Yesterday his remains were respectfully deposited in the New Presbyterian Burying Ground. (BMJ, 22 Jan. 1788)

HAYWARD, George Robins, of Talbot Co., married Thursday, 2nd inst., by Rev. Dr. Ferguson, to Peggy Smith of Kent Co. (EMH, 14 Dec. 1790)

HECK, Balser, of Frederick Town, dec.; Eve Margaret Heck, extx. (BMJ, 22 Oct. 1790) .

HELM, Mayberry, Sr., proposes to sell the tract of land where his son John lived and is now rented to Samuel Bond. (BMJ, 23 April 1790)

HELM, Mayberry, Sr., late of Baltimore Co., dec.; Leonard Helm, John McClellan, executors. (BMG, 24 Aug. 1790)

HENDERSON, Capt. Robert, of Fells Point, dec.; Elizabeth Henderson, extx. (BMG, 17 Dec. 1790)

HENRY, John, member of the Maryland Senate, married Tuesday, 6th inst.; Margaret Campbell of Dorchester Co. (BMJ, 30 March 1787)

HENRY, Mrs. Margaret, wife of the Hon. John Henry, died 11th inst., in her 23rd year. (BMG, 31 March 1789)

HIGGS, Ninean, of Anne Arundel Co., dec.; T. Bucknell, admin. (AMG, 17 Dec. 1789)

HILDEBRAND, Nicholas, late of Frederick Co., dec.; Mary Hildebrand, extx. (FMC, 15 Nov. 1786)

HILL, Benjamin, late master of the ship Pearce, dec.; Joseph Hill, admin. (BMJ, 19 Sept. 1786)

HILL, Joseph, Jr., of Anne Arundel Co., dec.; Joseph Hill, admin. (AMG, 6 May 1790)

HISER, Joshua, of Baltimore, will not pay the debts of his wife Sarah. (BMG, 16 Jan. 1787)

HOLLIDAY, Benoni, late of Anne Arundel Co., dec.; Richard Holliday, exec. (AMG, 21 Sept. 1786)

HOLLIDAY, Thomas, late of Anne Arundel Co., dec.; William Holliday, exec. (AMG, 21 Sept. 1786)

HOLLINGSWORTH, Mrs., consort of Jesse Hollingsworth, died Sunday night last. (BMJ, 5 Dec. 1786)

HOLLINGSWORTH, Miss, lines on her death in Jan. 1788. (BMJ, 12 Feb. 1788)

HOLLINGSWORTH, Horatio, died yesterday morning, aged 24 years, 6 months, son of Jesse Hollingsworth. (BMJ, 9 Feb. 1790)

HOLLINGSWORTH, Jesse, Esq., married Thursday evening last, Mrs. Rachel Parkin or Perkins, widow of the late Mr. Perkins, of Baltimore. (BMJ, 5 Oct. 1790; BMG, 5 Oct. 1790)

HOLLINGSWORTH, Zebulon, married last evening Betsy, daughter of Edward Ireland, merchant. (BMJ, 23 April 1790)

HOLLINS, John, merchant, married Saturday last in Baltimore, Jenny Smith, daughter of the Hon. John Smith. (BMG, 6 Jan. 1786)

HOLLINS, John, intends to embark for England next May. (BMG, 16 Jan. 1789)

HOLLIS, William, late of Harford Co., dec.; William Hollis, admin. (BMJ, 30 June 1786)

HOLLYDAY, James, died Sunday last in Queen Annes Co.; a lawyer and a statesman, and one of the framers of our Constitution. (BMJ, 10 Nov. 1786)

HOLMES, Eli, clerk to William Hammond, drowned Sunday. (BMG, 22 May 1787)

HONORE, Anthony, merchant, married Thursday, 31st ult., Mrs. Maria Meighan. (BMJ, 8 June 1787)

HOOD, John, late of Anne Arundel Co., dec.; Elizabeth Hood, John Hood, execs. (BMJ, 15 Aug. 1786)

HOOD, Zachariah, died Monday, 4th ult., at St. Georges, Bermuda, where he went for his health; the British agent for Turk's Island. He was a native of this state. (BMJ, 16 June 1789)

HOOPER, Henry, died suddenly, 3rd inst., at his seat in Dorchester Co. (BMJ, 15 Oct. 1790)

HOPKINS, Daniel, died Tuesday, 26th ult, at Elk Ridge, son of the Rev. Mr. Hopkins of Newport, R. I. (BMJ, 4 March 1788)

HOPKINS, Major David, married Saturday evening last, Polly, daughter of Edward Dorsey. (BMJ, 14 Dec. 1790)

HOPKINS, Philip, of Anne Arundel Co., died testate; Richard Hopkins will sell land of the deceased. (AMG, 2 April 1789) Two hundred acres of "Hopkins' Fancy," belonging to the deceased will be sold (AMG, 2 April 1789)

HOPKINS, Philip, dec.; Stephen West cautions all persons from buying Hopkins Fancy, as West has a conveyance for the tract from Gerard Hopkins, Elizabeth, widow of the late Philip Hopkins, the eldest son of Philip Hopkins, from Richard the second son, from Richard Dowell, who married a daughter of Philip Hopkins, and from Mr. Hutton who married another daughter of Philip. (AMG, 9 April 1789)

HOPKINSON, Rev. Mr. Thomas, died 26th May, aged between 30 and 40 years, at Cedar Hill, Charles Co., the seat of Dr. B. Fendall. (BMJ, 17 June 1788)

HOUSTON, Dr. James, late of Salisbury, Md., dec.; John P. Mitchell, admin. (BMJ, 3 August 1790)

HOWARD, Mrs., died Friday last at the house of George Salmon, in her 58th year. (BMG, 9 Jan. 1787)

HOWARD, Benjamin, late of Patapsco River, Anne Arundel Co.; Richard Ridgely and William Hammond, trustees. (AMG, 16 July 1789)

HOWARD, Benjamin, dec.; his dwelling house on Patapsco River will be the scene of a sale of 240 acres of "Yates Inheritance." (BMJ, 25 Aug. 1789)

HOWARD, Dr. Ephraim, lived near Elk Ridge Church, dec.; Achsah Howard, extx. (BMG, 2 Jan. 1789)

HOWARD, James, late of Anne Arundel Co., dec.; Ehpraim Howard of Joshua and Joshua Howard, execs. (BMJ, 31 March 1786)

HOWARD, Col. John E., of Baltimore, married at Philadelphia, Miss Chew, daughter of the Hon. Benjamin Chew, Esq. (BMJ, 12 June 1787)

HOWARD, Samuel, of Anne Arundel Co., dec.; Jemima Howard, admnx. (BMJ, 3 July 1787)

HOWARD, William, late of Frederick Co., dec.; Martha Howard, Cornelius Howard, execs. (FMC, 28 March 1787)

HOWELL, Jehu, a very ingenious architect of Baltimore Co., Md., drowned last
Friday morning, leaving a wife and two children. (BMJ, 27 Nov. 1787)

HUDSON, Jonathan, merchant of Baltimore, died suddenly at Upper Marlborough, a
husband and parent. (BMG, 12 Sept. 1786) Margaret Hudson, the widow, will
settle the estate. (BMG, 19 Sept. 1786)

HUDSON, Jonathan, of Baltimore, dec.; Mary Hudson, admnx. (BMJ, 23 March 1787)

HUDSON, V. John, denies he has two wives, let alone three. (BMJ, 23 Jan. 1789)
His only wife is Fanny, daughter of John and Sarah Nutbrown. (BMJ, 30
Jan. 1789)

HUGGINS, Thomas, merchant, died Wednesday last at Elkton, Cecil Co. (BMJ, 25
April 1788)

HUGHES, James, late of Cecil Co., dec.; Sarah Hughes, David Hairs, representatives
of the deceased. (BMJ, 26 Jan. 1790)

HUGHES, Capt. William, married a few days ago, Betsy M'Kirdy, daughter of Capt.
John M'Kirdy of Baltimore. (BMJ, 27 Nov. 1789)

HUMBERT, Michael, of Hagerstown; wife Elizabeth has eloped and taken two children
with her. (EWS, 7 Dec. 1790)

HUMPHREYS, Whitehead, died Saturday, 2nd inst., at Philadelphia; carried on manu-
facturing. (BMG, 12 Sept. 1786)

HUNT, John, of Baltimore Town, merchant, died suddenly Saturday morning last. The
next day his remains were interred in St. Paul's Churchyard, attended by his
Masonic brethren. (BMJ, 26 June 1787)

HUNTER, Peter, of Baltimore County, will petition the Assembly for an act to
recover a deed of conveyance for part of "Taylor's Discovery" on Winter's
Run, conveyed by Richard Wiley to Peter's father, William Hunter. (BMG,
26 Oct. 1787)

HUNTER, William, of Baltimore Co., dec.; Oliver Matthews has part of his estate
in his possession. (BMG, 19 Jan. 1790)

HUSBAND, Joseph, late of Harford Co., dec.; Joshua Husband, acting admin. (BMJ,
13 Oct. 1786)

HUSBAND, Joseph, dec.; over 300 acres of land in Harford Co. will be sold for
the benefit of his heirs. Anyone wishing to see the land should apply to
Joshua Husband or to John Stump. (BMJ, 13 Oct. 1789)

HUTCHINGS, Mrs. Catherine, died Wednesday last at Kent Island, Queen Annes Co.;
consort of James Hutchings, Esq. (BMJ, 22 Sept. 1789)

HUTCHINGS, John, (of Somerset Co.?), dec.; Thomas Newton, John Boush, admins.
(BMJ, 2 March 1790)

HUTCHINS, Capt. Thomas, dec.; John Rumsey, admin.

HYDE, William, late of Annapolis, dec.; William Goldsmith, admin. (AMG, 4 Jan.
1787)

HYNER, Nicholas, will not pay the debts of his wife Mary, who left his bed and
board in 1783 and lived with Patrick Kelly untill 1788 when Kelly died.
(BMG, 6 June 1788)

IAMS, Thomas, late of Annapolis, dec.; William Goldsmith is empowered to settle
the estate. (AMG, 9 Feb. 1786)

IJAMS, Thomas, late of Annapolis, dec.; Thomas Pyper, admin. (AMG, 9 Aug. 1787)

INNES, Rear Admiral Alexander, died on Sunday, 15th Jan., at the Government Pen
(sic), near Kingston, Jamaica. (BMJ, 7 March 1786)

IRELAND, Anna, died yesterday in her 19th year, eldest daughter of Edward Ireland
of Baltimore, merchant. (BMJ, 1 July 1788)

IRELAND, Gilbert, of Calvert Co., dec.; Eleanor Ireland, admnx. (AMG, 2 March
1786)

IRELAND, Gilbert, of Calvert Co., dec.; Rezin Estep, admin. (AMG, 13 March 1788)

IRELAND, Rev. John, married lately in Harford Co., Miss Nancy Waters. (BMJ, 2
Oct. 1787)

IRELAND, Thomas, late of Calvert Co., dec.; David Lock Weems, Daniel Kent,
execs. (AMG, 31 Dec. 1789)

IRVINE, Charles Edward, late of Caroline Co., dec.; Francis Sellers, admin.
(EMH, 1 June 1790)

JACKSON, Abraham, died last Friday morning, an ingenious useful mechanic. His
remains were interred on Sunday evening in St. Paul's Churchyard, attended by
his Masonic brethren. (BMJ, 30 Oct. 1787) Ann Jackson and William Jackson,
execs. (BMJ, 8 Feb. 1788 extraordinary)

JACOBS, George, of Prince Georges Co., dec.; Marsh M. Duvall, administrator de
bonis non. (AMG, 22 Jan. 1789)

JACOBS, Isaac, of Prince Georges Co., dec.; Marsh M. Duvall, admin. de bonis non. (AMG, 22 Jan. 1789)

JAMES, Capt. Jesse, late of Baltimore Town, dec.; George James, admin. (BMJ, 24 Nov. 1786)

JAMES, John, of the Fork of Gunpowder, will not pay the debts of his wife Mary. (BMJ, 31 Oct. 1786)

JAMES, John, a respectable inhabitant of Fells Point, died 27 Feb. (BMG, 4 March 1788)

JAMES, Dr. Thomas, dec.; left a widow Ann James. (BMJ, 4 May 1790)

JAMISON, Capt. Adam, of Baltimore, married Sunday evening, Polly Johnson, daughter of Thomas Johnson, of Baltimore Co. (BMG, 12 Sept. 1786)

JEANIN, M., from France, offers his services as a dentist. (BMJ, 9 March 1787)

JEFFRIES, Robert, late of Harford Co., dec.; Elizabeth Jeffries, extx. (BMG, 17 Sept. 1790)

JENIFER, Daniel of St. Thomas, died early in the morning of the 16th inst., in his 67th year. (BMJ, 19 Nov. 1790)

JENIFER, Dr. Walter Harrison, late of Charles Co., dec.; Daniel Jenifer, Daniel Jenifer, Jr., execs. (AMG, 16 Feb. 1786)

JOHNS, Capt. Richard, married Thursday evening (the 9th inst.), Polly Luce. (BMJ, 17 April 1789)

JOHNSON, John, late of Annapolis, dec.; Robert Johnson, admin. (AMG, 26 March 1789)

JOHNSON, Thomas, late of the Cliffs, Calvert Co., dec.; Mary Cleaverly Johnson, extx. (AMG, 11 Jan. 1787)

JONES, Henry, of Anne Arundel Co., dec.; Thomas Harwood, exec. (AMG, 2 Nov. 1786)

JONES, Richard, of Baltimore, will not pay the debts of his wife Eleanor. (BMG, 13 July 1790)

JONES, Thomas, of Baltimore Co., dec.; blacksmith John Townsley, exec. (BMJ, 26 Dec. 1788)

JORDAN, Capt. John, late of Charles Co., dec.; John Thomas, admin. (AMG, 23 April 1789)

JORDAN, Justinian, late of St. Marys Co., dec.; Jeremiah Jordan, Charles Lewellin, execs. (AMG, 1 Oct. 1789)

KELL, Jupiter, will not pay the debts of his wife Ruth. (BMG, 23 Sept. 1788)

KELL, Capt. Thomas, lately died at Guadeloupe, late of Baltimore. (BMJ, 15 Oct. 1790)

KELSO, John, died Wednesday last, second son of Mr. James Kelso, merchant of Baltimore. (BMG, 3 Oct. 1786)

KENNEDY, Joseph, stucco-workman, plasterer, and plain painter from Dublin, has settled in Baltimore, and carries on his profession. He has a letter from H. D. Gough at Perry Hall, recommending him. (BMJ, 6 Oct. 1789)

KEY, Philip, advertises for the return of a gilt watch with a seal bearing the family crest: a griffin's head with a key in its beak, and the motto: Faithful, More Faithful. (BMJ, 4 Sept. 1787)

KIEFER, Frederick, fell and broke his neck last Friday night, walking on Church Hill. (BMJ, 20 June 1786)

KILLEN, Mrs. Mary, died Saturday evening last in her 25th year, wife of John Killen, merchant; her remains were interred in the Reformed German Burying Ground. (BMJ, 29 Sept. 1789)

KING, Henry, late of Prince Georges Co., dec.; Robert Sim, admin. (AMG, 23 Nov. 1786)

KING, Samuel, Esq., died 24th November last, at his seat in Somerset Co. (BMJ, 24 Dec. 1790)

KINKEAD, John, married 21 Dec. 1786 at Charlestown, Mrs. Hambleton. "Cecil - 21 Dec. 1786." (BMJ, 26 Dec. 1786)

KIRK, James, died at Alexandria, late Mayor of that   borough. (BMJ, 11 April 1786)

KIRWAN, John, merchant of Baltimore, married Polly Sewell of St. Marys Co. (BMJ, 28 Feb. 1786)

KITTEMAN, George, of Liberty Town, will not pay the debts of his wife Charlotte who has eloped. (BMJ, 23 June 1789)

KLEIMENHAGEN, William, advertises he came from Waldeck, Upper Waroldern, Germany, and had a brother John Henry Kleimenhagen, who may be living in Baltimore. William is living with Abraham Kegy of Lancaster Co., Penna. (BMJ, 10 April 1789)

KOONTZ, Jacob, of Frederick Co., will not pay the debts of his wife Mary. (FMC, 4 July 1787)

KURTS, Rev. Mr. Daniel, married Sunday evening last, Polly, daughter of Samuel Messersmith of this town. (BMG, 10 Sept. 1790)

LAMBDIN, Daniel, late of Talbot Co., dec.; Joseph Harrison, III, exec. (EMH, 21 Sept. 1790)

LANE, Capt. Richard, dec.; Providence Lane, extx. (BMJ, 7 Aug. 1787)

LANGLY, Sarah, formerly Helems, intends to petition the Assembly for a tract "Resurvey on Charleymount," to be the property of Thomas Helems, minor, son of Joseph Helems, dec. (FMC, 13 Sept. 1786)

LANSDALE, Jeremiah, of Prince Georges Co., died a few days ago, at the house of Mr. S. Sadler in Baltimore. Lansdale was studying law in Baltimore. (BMJ, 22 May 1787)

LARGEAU, Mrs. Rachel, died Tuesday night, aged 23 years, wife of George James Largeau, and daughter of William Adams. Her remains were deposited in St. Pauls Churchyard last evening. (BMJ, 27 March 1789)

LATIL, Mrs. Lucy, died at Richmond, Va., on Sat., 16th inst., consort of Joseph Latil, merchant, formerly a resident of Baltimore. (BMJ, 26 Jan. 1790)

LATSHAW, John, late an inhabitant of Baltimore Town, left this place on a business trip last August intending to be gone only a month. His wife Magdalena advertises for knowledge of his whereabouts. (BMJ, 24 Jan. 1786) Latshaw was barbarously murdered some time last November in Bladen Co., N. C., on his way home to Baltimore. (BMJ, 21 Feb. 1786)

LAWLER, Mary, otherwise Phelar, arrived in Baltimore in 1774 or 1775, daughter of Richard Lawler of Stradbally, Ireland. She is urged to contact the printer. (BMG, 24 Nov. 1789)

LAZENBY, Robert, late of Montgomery Co.; John Lazenby, exec. (BMJ, 13 Jan. 1786)

LEARY, Daniel, of Baltimore, died Tuesday evening, as a result of a fall down into the hold of the ship Chesapeake on Sunday. He leaves a wife and five children. (BMJ, 13 Aug. 1790)

LECKE, Francis, late of P. G. Co., dec.; Anne Lecke, admnx. (BMJ, 4 June 1790)

LEE, Edward, late of Anne Arundel Co., dec.; Mary Lee and Solomon Sparrow, admins. (AMG, 12 Jan. 1786)

LEE, Mrs. Grace, relict of the Hon. Richard Lee, died at Blenheim, 16th ult., aged about 76 years. (BMG, 3 Nov. 1789)

LEE, the Hon. Richard, died at Blenheim, Charles Co., on 26th Jan., in his 81st year. He leaves a wife to whom he has been married for over 50 years. (BMJ, 16 Feb. 1787) Grace Lee, Alice Lee, admins. (AMG, 20 Dec. 1787) Philip R. Fendall, admin. de bonis non. (BMJ, 27 Nov. 1789)

LEE, Miss Sidney, died 16th Jan. last in Chester, Eng.; sister of the late Gen. Charles Lee. She gave unsolicited contributions for the support and comfort of American prisoners in England during the late war. (BMJ, 15 April 1788)

LEECHMAN, Rev. William, D. D., died in Scotland, at an advanced age; Principal of the University of Glasgow. (BMJ, 17 Feb. 1786)

LEEKE, Frank, merchant, died a7th Feb. at Upper Marlborough, Prince Georges Co. (BMJ, 26 March 1790) Anne Leeke, admnx. (AMG, 27 May 1790)

LENOX, Mrs. Ruth, late of Baltimore Co., dec.; Orlando G. Dorsey, exec. (BMJ, 19 Feb. 1790)

LEOPOLD, Charles, of Baltimore, advertises his wife's repeated elopements. (BMJ, 30 Jan. 1787)

LEVELY, William, tavernkeeper, died a few days ago. (BMJ, 14 Sept. 1787) Catherine Levely, extx. (BMJ, 26 Jan. 1790)

LEVY, Mr. Herman, died Wednesday, 19th inst.; merchant of New York, and one of the Hebrew religion. (BMG, 28 Aug. 1789)

LIEUTAUD, John, gardener and florist from France, offers his goods. He lives at Capt. Gould's in Charles St., where a printed catalog may be seen. He also has a good collection of natural curiosities from Dauphiny. (BMJ, 2 April 1790)

LIGGAT, Samuel, merchant of Baltimore, married a few days ago at Frederick, Jenny Parks, daughter of John Parks, merchant. (BMJ, 25 Dec. 1787)

LIGGAT, Samuel, merchant of Baltimore, died Tuesday last (29th ult.) at Frederick Town, in his 25th year, leaving a young wife. (BMJ, 2 Oct. 1789) Jane Liggat admnx. (BMJ, 27 Oct. 1789)

LINCOLN, Benjamin, died at Boston, 18th inst., attorney at law, aged 29 years, son to the Hon. Major General Lincoln; "New York, 29 Jan." (BMJ, 8 Feb. 1788)

LINGAN, Nicholas, of Georgetown, merchant, married 5th inst., at Green Hill, Charles Co., Anna, daughter of Samuel Hanson, Esq. (BMJ, 30 Oct. 1789)

LITHGOW, Hector, about 1764 was a private in H. B. M. 77th Regt., then quartered at Halifax, N. S.; he left for Great Britain, and then went to the East

Indies, where he died in 1784. He left a considerable property to his sons John and Hugh Lithgow, and their mother Frances Sweeting. Hugh Lithgow is supposed to be in some part of the Eastern Shore of Maryland, where he married some years ago. (BMJ, 1 Aug. 1788)

LITTIG, Yoist, late of Baltimore Town, dec.; Philip Littig, admin. (BMJ, 24 Feb. 1786)

LIVINGSTON, William, died Sunday, 25th inst., at his seat near Elizabethtown, N. J., Governor of that state. (EMH, 17 Aug. 1790)

LLOYD, Richard Bennett, late of Queen Annes Co., dec.; James Hindman, admin. (AMG, 27 March 1788)

LOCKLEY, John, a native of England, died in Va., at Mr. Rockett's. (BMJ, 14 Feb. 1786)

LOUTTIT, James, died early this morning of 8th inst., at his seat in Sassafras Neck, Cecil Co. (BMJ, 23 Dec. 1788)

LOWE, Col. John Hawkins, late of Prince Georges Co., dec.; Barbara Lowe, admnx., has empowered John Read Magruder to settle the estate. (AMG, 24 July 1788)

LOWE, Thomas, son of Edward and Mary Lowe of Marylebone, London, came to Md. about 35 years ago with his uncles John and Robert Chesley. He should apply to Zachariah Forrest. (AMG, 9 March 1786)

LOWES, Mr. Tubman, married Thursday, 9th inst., in Calvert Co., Betsy Bond. (BMJ, 17 April 1789)

LOWNDES, Benjamin, of Bladensburg, married Thursday, 28th ult., in Baltimore Co., Dorothy Buchanan, daughter of the late George Buchanan. (BMJ, 5 Nov. 1790)

LOWNDES, Mrs. Elizabeth, died Saturday, 19th inst., at Bladensburg, relict of the late Christopher Lowndes, Esq. (BMJ, 25 Sept. 1789)

LUCAS, Col. Barton, late of Prince Georges Co., dec.; Joseph Sprigg will petition the General Assembly to confirm the deceased's will. (AMG, 5 Jan. 1786)

LUCKETT, Thomas Hussey, late of Loudon Co., Va., dec.; Elizabeth Luckett, extx. (BMJ, 9 Feb. 1787)

LUSBY, Baldwin, late of Anne Arundel Co., dec.; Robert Lusby, exec. (AMG, 21 May 1789)

LUSBY, Delia, late of South River, Anne Arundel Co., dec.; Eliza Murdocks, admin. (AMG, 28 Oct. 1790)

LUSBY, John, late of Baltimore Co., dec.; Jasper Edward Tully, admin. (AMG, 17 Dec. 1789)

LUX, Mrs. Catherine, wife of Mr. George Lux of Chatsworth, near this town, died; daughter of the late Edward Biddle of Reading, Penna. (BMJ, 16 Feb. 1790)

LYLES, Walter, late of Calvert Co., dec.; Mary Lyles, extx. (AMG, 18 Nov. 1790)

LYON, Hugh, of Prince Georges Co., dec.; John Beall, admin. (AMG, 25 Oct. 1787)

McBRIDE, Hugh, respectable merchant of Baltimore, died Friday evening last. His remains were interred in the Presbyterian graveyard. (BMG, 19 June 1787) D. Williamson, admin. (BMJ, 3 Aug. 1787)

McCANNON, John, died in Baltimore. (BMJ, 29 April 1788)

McCARDLE, Patrick, of Hagerstown, Washington Co., dec.; Nathaniel Morgan, William Heyser, admins. (BMJ, 29 Sept. 1786)

McCARTY, Jacob Giles, of Baltimore Co., will petition the Assembly to make valid the will of Samuel McCarty. (BMJ, 1 April 1788)

McCAULEY, Zachariah, late of Anne Arundel Co., dec.; Anne McCauley, now wife of William Bird, admin. (AMG, 19 March 1789)

McCLELIAN, Col. David, died 2nd inst., at his house in Marsh Creek Settlement, York Co., Penna. (BMJ, 26 March 1790)

McFADON, Capt. James, died Friday morning last in his 33rd year. He commanded a company in the late American army and proved himself a brave and faithful officer. On Sunday afternoon his remains were deposited in the Presbyterian graveyard and attended by the Masonic brethren. (BMJ, 19 Oct. 1790)

McHENRY, John, died 7th inst., aged 35 years, merchant of this town. (BMJ, 11 May 1790)

MACKINTOSH, James, lost his life in the late calamitous inundation (mentioned in our last issue). Barely 20 years old, he was a native of Scotland. He was buried in the Presbyterian New Burying Ground. (BMJ, 29 July 1788)

McCOMSEY, Robert, of Baltimore Co., will not pay the debts of his wife Catherine. (BMJ, 4 Aug. 1786)

MACCUBBIN, Nicholas, son of Joseph, late of Annapolis, dec.; Sarah Maccubbin, extx. (AMG, 2 March 1786)

McELDERRY, Thomas, merchant of Baltimore, married Saturday evening last, Betsy, dau. of John Parks, merchant. (BMG, 19 June 1787)

MacGILL, Rev. Mr. James, dec.; Sarah MacGill, admnx. (AMG, 9 March 1786)

MacGILL, John, died Friday morning last at his seat near Fredericktown in his
53rd year. (FMC, 10 May 1786) John MacGill, Patrick MacGill, execs.
(AMG, 14 Sept. 1786) The notice mentions property formerly held by the
late Rev. James MacGill. (AMG, 21 Sept. 1786)

M'IVER, Colin, merchant, died last Tuesday, in his 33rd year; a native of Scotland; "Alexandria, Dec. 10." (BMJ, 15 Jan. 1788)

MACKY, Capt. William, late of the city of Dublin, dec.; John Norwood, admin.
(BMG, 16 May 1786)

M'KURDY, John, died Sunday last, son of Capt. John M'Kurdy of Baltimore. (BMG,
2 Dec. 1788)

M'IAUGHLIN, William, married by Rev. Dr. West, Polly, daughter of the late Jonathan Plowman, Esq. (BMJ, 23 Jan. 1787) (BMG, 23 Jan. 1787)

McPARIANE, John, late tutor in the family of Michael Taney, died. (BMG, 12 Nov.
1790)

M'PHERSON, Mrs. Mary Fendall, died Thursday, 4th inst., at the house of Samuel
H. McPherson, near Port Tobacco, Charles Co., in her 30th year; wife of
Walter McPherson, Jr.; "Georgetown, 13 Nov.", (BMJ, 19 Nov. 1790)

McSHERRY, Patrick, of York Co., Penna., married Sunday evening last, Betsy Clements
of Baltimore. (BMJ, 13 April 1790)

MADDOCKE, Notley, of Charles Co., dec.; his sons Notley and Henry advertise they
intend to take depositions to establish their father's last will and testa-
ment. (AMG, 22 Feb. 1787)

MAGOWAN, Rev. Walter, late of St. James' Parish; William Steuart, John Weems,
admins. (AMG, 15 Feb. 1787)

MAGRUDER, Enoch, late of Broad Creek, dec.; D. Magruder, exec. (AMG, 2 Nov.
1786)

MAGRUDER, Mrs. Mary, wife of Nathaniel Jones Magruder, will petition the Assembly
to secure to her use sundry negroes devised to her by her father John
Billingsby, in order to prevent her said husband from depriving her of the
use of the said negroes. (AMG, 15 Oct. 1789)

MARARLE, John, died in Mecklenburg, Va. (BMJ, 18 April 1786)

MARKELL, John, of Baltimore, will not pay the debts of his wife Sarah as she is
"led by the persuasions of her father and other people who I think might
mind their business and look at home." (BMJ, 23 May 1786)

MARVELL, Francis, late of Baltimore Town, dec.; Mary Marvell, admnx. (BMJ, 21 April 1789) Mary Marvell is trustee for Rebecca Marvell. (BMJ, 6 Nov. 1789)

MATTHEWS, Daniel, of Fells Point, drowned last Saturday night, when he fell out of a boat in our harbor. (BMJ, 10 Oct. 1786)

MATTHEWS, James, late of Harford Co., dec.; Philip and Rebecca Henderson, admins. (BMJ, 2 Oct. 1787)

MAXWELL, James, late of Frederick Co., dec.; Margaret Maxwell, extx. (BMG, 16 Jan. 1787)

MAY, Henry, late of Anne Arundel Co., dec.; Richard Beard, Jr., exec. (AMG, 12 Feb. 1789)

MAY, Mrs. Rebecca Grace, died Thursday morning, 30th ult., in her 30th year, consort of Robert May of Cecil Co., Md. She was buried in the Burying Ground at Elkton. (BMJ, 28 Aug. 1789)

MAYERS, Frederick, tanner, of Baltimore Town, dec.; Michael Diffenderfer, Baltzer Shaeffer, execs. (BMG, 24 Nov. 1786). He died a few days ago in Baltimore at an advanced age. (BMJ, 24 Nov. 1786)

MAYO, John,, late of Anne Arundel Co., dec.; James Mayo, exec. (AMG, 7 May 1789)

MAYO, Joseph, late of Anne Arundel Co., dec.; Hannah Mayo, extx. (BMJ, 8 Aug. 1788)

MENTZ, Daniel, lived near the causeway leading to Fells Point. On Sunday evening last during a violent storm, lightning entered the house by the chimney and killed his venerable wife Elizabeth, daughter Pamela and son Jehu. An eight year old boy and his brother werev the only ones spared. (BMJ, 8 July 1788)

MERCER, John, dec.; his widow Susannah intends to petition the Assembly. (AMG, 31 Aug. 1786)

MERCER, John, advertises the loss of a cane with a coat of arms at the top and the motto "Non Nobis Solum," and the latters "I. A." (AMG, 29 Jan. 1789)

MERCER, Mrs. Rebecca, consort of Peregrine Mercer, died Monday last in Anne Arundel Co. (BMJ, 27 Oct. 1786)

MESSONIER, Mrs. Elizabeth, died Tuesday evening last, consort of Henry Messonier merchant, and daughter of Dr. Charles F. Wiessenthal. (BMG, 2 Nov. 1787)

MEYERS, Jacob, died Tuesday last, 2nd Oct., after a long and most painful illness. (BMG, 5 Oct. 1787) Margaret Meyer, Charles Meyer, Thomas Yates, execs. (BMG, 16 Oct. 1787)

MIDDLETON, James, late of Chas. Co., dec.; Ignatius Middleton, exec. (AMG, 21 Oct. 1790)

MIFFLIN, John, Jr., of Cecil Co., merchant, married 5th inst. at Woodbine, York Co., Penna., Miss Ewing, only daughter of Gen. Ewing. (BMJ, 25 May 1790)

MILES, James, son of John, of St. Marys Co., intends petitioning the Assembly for a law authorizing the justices of the county aforesaid to assess a sum of money yearly for his support. (AMG, 28 Oct. 1790)

MILLER, Catherine, daughter of Adam Miller of Bucks Co., Penna., went away with Jacob Conrad into Md. or Va. about 14 or 15 years ago. She should apply to John Weaver or Conrad Sherman. (BMG, 26 Feb. 1788)

MOALE, Richard, of Baltimore, died Wednesday afternoon. (BMG, 24 Feb. 1786) Frances H. Moale, John Moale, J. T. Chase, execs. (BMJ, 11 April 1786) John Moale, David Harris, and Frances Harris, execs. (BMJ, 25 May 1790)

MOHLER, Elizabeth, dec.; James Calhoun, Jacob Mohler, will settle the estate. (BMJ, 12 Oct. 1787)

MONTGOMERY, John, died Thursday night last at Fells Point. His remains were interred in the R. C. Churchyard. (BMJ, 31 March 1789)

MOODY, Moynes, late of Baltimore, dec.; Robert Slater, James Long, admins. (BMJ, 17 Oct. 1786) Hugh Moody, admin. de bonis non. (BMJ, 9 Jan. 1787)

MOORE, George, of Alexandria, Va., married Sunday evening last, Lydia Winchester, daughter of William Winchester of Baltimore. (BMJ, 28 Dec. 1790)

MOORE, James, son of Acheson Moore of Aughnacloy, Co. Tyrone, Ireland, should apply to the printers. (BMJ, 7 Sept. 1790)

MOORE, Robert, died early Wednesday morning, aged 64 years. His remains are to be interred early this afternoon in the New Presbyterian Burying Ground. He was a senior member of the ancient and honorable fraternity of Freemasons. (BMG, 16 Nov. 1787) Susanna Moore, admnx. (BMJ, 4 Dec. 1787)

MORRILL, Dr. James, of Switzerland, informs the inhabitants of Baltimore that he has just arrived from London. (BMJ, 24 Aug. 1790)

MORRIS, John, will not pay the debts of his wife Betty. (FMC, 14 June 1786)

MORRISON, Samuel, merchant, late of Baltimore Town, dec.; John Mickle and David Poe, admins. (BMG, 24 Jan. 1786)

MOSS, James, will not pay any debts of Monikey Moss. (AMG, 30 Oct. 1788)

MUMMA, Barbara, will petition the Assembly for a law to prevent her husband, David Mumma, from conveying his property away from his wife and children. (BMJ, 20 Oct. 1789)

MUMMY, Benjamin, Sr., of Baltimore Co., will not pay the debts of his wife Barbary. (BMJ, 10 Nov. 1786)

MURPHY, William, intends to leave for Europe shortly. (BMJ, 2 Jan. 1787)

MURRAY, John, late of Baltimore Co., dec.; his 91 acre tract near Reisterstown was seized and taken at the suit of the State of Maryland, and will be sold by Thomas Rutter, sheriff. (BMJ, 29 May 1789) His property which was siezed at the suit of George Ashman will be sold Wednesday, 14th April, at Mrs. Murray's in Reisterstown. (BMJ, 13 April 1790)

MURRAY, John, merchant of Elkton, Cecil Co., died 7th inst. as a result of a fall from a carriage the previous evening. (BMJ, 17 Sept. 1790)

MURRAY, Mrs. Mary, died Wednesday morning last in Baltimore, wife of Edward Murray, merchant. Her remains will be interred this day at 3:00 P. M. in St. Paul's Churchyard. (BMJ, 26 Nov. 1790)

MYERS, Charles, merchant of Baltimore, married Betsy, only daughter of the late Capt. Thomas Jarold of this place. (BMJ, 2 Jan. 1787)

MYERS, Jacob, late of Baltimore Town, dec.; Margaret Myers, Charles Myers, Thomas Yates, execs. The notice gives a description of the property of the deceased. (BMJ, 18 Aug. 1788)

NEILL, Mrs. Elizabeth, died Tuesday last at Fredericktown, consort of Mr. John Neill of that place, merchant. (BMJ, 7 April 1786)

NEILL, William, merchant of Baltimore, dec.; Hercules Courtenay, acting exec., also dec.; (BMG, 3 Jan. 1786) Hercules Courtenay and Isabella, wife of Thomas M'Intire, execs. (BMJ, 10 June 1788)

NICHOLS, Elisha, labouring man, drowned yesterday when a bank he was digging near Jones Falls gave way and fell on him. (BMJ, 27 March 1789)

NICHOLS, Thomas, late of Anne Arundel Co., dec.; was appointed inspector of Chaptico warehouse in 1782. (AMG, 22 Feb. 1787) Jean Nicholas, admnx. (AMG, 12 April 1787)

NICHOLSON, John, of Baltimore, merchant, married Sunday, 26th ult., Susanna Peachey, daughter of Col. William Peachey of Milden Hall, Richmond Co., Va. (BMJ, 8 May 1789)

NOEL, Mrs. Ruth, wife of Capt. Septimus Noel, died Sunday morning last, at an advanced age. (BMJ, 3 April 1787)

NOON, William, late of Baltimore, dec.; James Edwards, Abraham Scott, execs. (BMJ, 28 July 1789)

NORRIS, Benjamin Bradford, died a few days ago after a short illness aged about 40 years, late one of the representatives of Harford Co. in the state legislature. (BMJ, 19 March 1790)

NORRIS, Joseph, late of Harford Co., dec.; Nathan Gallion, Christian Gallion, execs. (BMJ, 22 Feb. 1788 - extraordinary issue)

OLDHAM, Major Edward, died last week at Bohemia Manor, Cecil Co.,...an honest patriot and a brave soldier. (BMG, 19 June 1787) Note - the account of his death is premature. (BMG, 26 June 1787)

OWEN, James, of Montgomery Co., dec.; Samuel Brooke, admin. (BMJ, 16 Feb. 1790)

OWEN, Robert, tavern keeper, late of Frederick, dec.; Rebecca Owen, admnx. (FMC, 28 June 1786)

OWENS, James, late of Anne Arundel Co., dec.; Anne Owens, James Owens, execs. (AMG, 21 Dec. 1786)

OWINGS, Christopher, late of Baltimore Co., dec.; Benjamin Lawrence, Bale Owings, admins. (BMJ, 13 Oct. 1786)

OWINGS, Mrs. Frances, wife of Nicholas Owings, merchant of Baltimore, died in Baltimore Co. (BMJ, 29 April 1788)

OWINGS, Nicholas, merchant of this town, married Fanny Risteau, of Baltimore Co. (BMJ, 24 Feb. 1786)

OWINGS, Richard, late of Baltimore Co., dec.; Rachel Owings, John Beasman, execs. (BMJ, 26 Dec. 1786) Richard Owings had lived in Upper Delaware Hundred. (BMJ, 11 Jan. 1788)

OWINGS, Major Robert, late of Montgomery County, near head of Seneca, dec.; Benjamin D. Penn, admin. (BMG, 20 July 1787)

PACA, Aquila, died 26th ult. at his house in Abingdon, Harford Co. (BMJ, 29 Feb. 1788) Helen Paca, extx. (BMJ, 8 April 1788)

PACKER, George, late of Anne Arundel Co., dec.; Mary Packer, admnx. (AMG, 18 May 1786)

PAINE, Mrs. Elizabeth, relict of William Paine of this town, died Saturday
    evening last, aged 74. (BMG, 1 June 1787)

PARKE, John, Esq., formerly a lieutenant-colonel in the army of the United
    States, died 24 Jan. last, in Queen Annes Co. (BMJ, 8 April 1788)

PARKER, Col. Edward, late of Cecil Co., dec.; Joseph Parker, exec. Margery
    Parker, Joseph Parker, Robert Parker, devisees; notice contains description
    of property. (BMJ, 25 Aug. 1789)

PARKER, Jonathan, late of Annapolis, dec.; Rachel Parker will settle the estate.
    (AMG, 7 Sept. 1786)

PARKINSON, Capt. Edward, late of Fells Point, dec.; Diana Parkinson, admnx.
    (BMJ, 28 March 1786)

PARKS, William, states thatb his father, when still living, gave a bond to a cer-
    tain Joshua Cockey, late of Baltimore Co., dec., for a tract of land called
    "Parks' Deathnot." If the heirs of the said Cockey will produce the bond,
    Parks will convey the land. (BMJ, 23 Oct. 1789)

PARRAN, Young, of Calvert Co., dec.; died leaving part of sour tracts of land:
    "Nutts Cliffts," "Chaplin," and East Chaplin," and "Meares" to his son
    John, who is now also dec.; the land has passed to the heir at law of
    John. (AMG, 3 April 1788)

PARTRIDGE, Francis, late of Baltimore, merchant, married 19th ult., at Elkton,
    Hannah, daughter of the Hon. Joseph Gilpin. (BMJ, 8 Dec. 1789)

PATRICK, Mrs. Elizabeth, died on Sunday morning last, consort of John Patrick
    of Baltimore. (BMJ, 4 April 1786)

PATRICK, George, of Harford Co., Md., will not pay the debts of his wife Ruth,
    who has eloped from his bed and board. (YPH, 8 Sept. 1790)

PATTERSON, John, late of Harford Co., dec.; George Patterson, admin. (BMJ, 27
    Feb. 1787)

PATTISON, Richard, late of Dor. Co., dec.; James Pattison of William, exec.
    (AMG, 25 Dec. 1788)

PEARCE, William, died testate; Henry Ward Pearce, admin. (BMJ, 15 June 1787)

PERRY, Mrs., died 5th inst., at Sweet Springs, Botetourt Co., Va., wife of William
    Perry of Talbot Co., Md. (BMJ, 25 Sept. 1789)

PERRY, Hon. William, married Sunday, 21st inst., in Talbot Co., Sally Rule. (BMJ,
    30 Oct. 1787)

PHELPS, Capt. John Parker, married Thursday evening last, Hannah Jacobs, daughter of William Jacobs of Fells Point. (BMG, 5 Jan. 1790)

PHILLIPS, Capt. James, died Saturday last, in his 51st year, a native of New England, but for many years past a resident of Baltimore. On Sunday his remains were deposited in the New Presbyterian Burying Ground, attended by his Masonic brethren. (BMJ, 14 April 1789) Bethiah Phillips, admnx. (BMJ, 15 Sept. 1789)

PICKETT, George, married a few days ago at Richmond, Va., Mrs. Margaret Flint, late of Baltimore. (BMJ, 3 Nov. 1789)

PIERCE, Humphrey, merchant, married Nancy Williamson, both of Baltimore. (BMJ, 7 Aug. 1789)

PIERPOINT, Charles, late of Baltimore Co., dec.; Joseph Pierpoint, Amos Pierpoint, execs. (BMJ, 16 June 1786)

PINDELL, John, of Baltimore Co., wife Eleanor has elpped. (BMG, 20 Jan. 1786)

PINDELL, John, late of Baltimore Co., dec.; John Pindell, Jr., exec. (BMJ, 29 Sept. 1789)

PINE, Mrs. Mary, wife of John Pine, of Fells Point, died Sunday morning last, in her 57th year. Last evening her remains were interred in St. Pauls' Churchyard. (BMJ, 24 Aug. 1790)

PIPER, William, late of Baltimore Town, dec.; widow Elizabeth Piper; Abraham Larsch, exec. (BMJ, 27 July 1787)

PLAISTED, Mary, challenges the allegations of her husband, Mordecai, that she ran him into debt. (BMJ, 19 March 1790)

PLOWDEN, Francis G., late of St. Marys Co., dec.; Edmund Plowden, Henry Neale, execs. (AMG, 18 Sept. 1788)

PLOWMAN, Jonathan, of Baltimore, dec.; Robert Ballard, admin. (BMG, 20 April 1787) Plowman died owner of a dwelling house and lot on the east side of Jones Falls, plus assorted tracts of land. He left a son and heir Jonathan. Edward Johnson and William M'Laughlin, trustees, advertise a sale of property. (BMJ, 26 Oct. 1787)

POOL, William, of Anne Arundel Co., will not pay the debts of his wife Anne. (BMJ, 10 Feb. 1786)

PORTNEY, Thomas, of Alexandria, merchant, married 21st inst., at Montgomery Co. Friends Meeting House, Nancy, daughter of Evan Thomas. (BMJ, 27 April 1790)

PORTTEUS, Robert, late of Baltimore, dec.; John Weatherburn, exec. (BMG, 2 Jan. 1787)

POWELL, Benjamin, late of Baltimore, dec.; John Hayward, exec., advertises that the tract, part of "Molly's and Sally's Delight," will be sold. (BMJ, 27 Oct. 1789)

PRATTEN, Thomas, of Baltimore, died Thursday last. His remains were interred on Saturday evening in the German Lutheran Church. (BMG, 17 Oct. 1786) Caroline Pratten, admnx. (BMJ, 31 Oct. 1786)

PRESS, Henry, baker, late of Fells Point, dec.; Jacob Brown, George Rease, admins. (BMG, 7 March 1786)

PRICE, Major Jacob, of the Maryland Line, died 25 Dec. 1789 at Savannah, Ga. (Scharf, History of Baltimore City and County, pp. 805, 806)

PRICE, Milisent, late of Baltimore Co., dec.; Thomas Price, Christopher Vaughan, exeгs. (BMG, 21 March 1788)

PROCTOR, John, painter, died last Wednesday, aged 45. He was a native of old England. Funeral from his house in Market St. (BMJ, 31 Dec. 1790) His remains will be interred in St. Pauls Churchyard. (BMG, 31 Dec. 1790)

PROCTOR, Mrs. Margaret, died Friday last, in her 34th year, wife of John Proctor of Baltimore, painter. Her remains were interred in St. Pauls Church yard. (BMG, 8 Dec. 1789)

PURVIANCE, Mrs. Mary, widow of the late Samuel Purviance, merchant, formerly of Philadelphia, died at her farm in Salem Co., West Jersey, on Tuesday, 27 Jan., aged 76. (BMG, 24vFeb. 1789)

RAMSEY, Mrs. Margaret Jane, wife of the Hon. Nathaniel Ramsey, died Friday last in Cecil Co. (BMJ, 4 Jan. 1788)

RAMSEY, Nathaniel, Marshal of Md., married lately in Harford Co., Charlotte, daughter of the late Aquila Hall of that county. (BMJ, 9 Feb. 1790)

RAMSEY, Mrs. M Jane, died Friday, 28 Dec., near Charlestown, Cecil Cб., consort of Col. Nathaniel Ramsey. Her remains were interred at Northeast Church. (BMG, 4 Jan. 1788)

RAPP, Dr. Frederick, from Strasburg, lately from Philadelphia, practices physic, surgery, and midwifery. (AMG, 21 May 1789)

RAWLINS, Jonathan, of Anne Arundel Co., dec.; Richard Rawlings, exec. (AMG, 22 Oct. 1789) Gassaway Rawlings admin. de bonis non. (AMG, 4 March 1790)

RAWLINS, John, died Thursday last, aged 42 years, an "ingenuous and honest tradesman." (BMG, 31 July 1787) Johnzee Sellman, admin., advertises a sale of household goods. (BMJ, 4 Sept. 1787)

RAY, Richard, will not pay the debts of his wife Elizabeth who has eloped from his bed and board. (EMH, 21 Dec. 1790)

READER, Dr. Henry, late of St. M. Co., dec.; Elizabeth Reader and Thomas A. Reader, execs. (AMG, 10 May

REED, Capt. James, married Tuesday eve., 13th inst., Nelly Taylor of Balto. (BMJ, 23 April 1790)

REEHM, Christopher, late of Balto. Town, dec.; Catherine Reehm, admnx. (BMG, 4 May 1787)

REES, David, merchant, of Balto., married Thursday last, by Rev. Mr. Emerson, at Portsmouth, Mrs. Mary Rothery. (BMJ, 25 Nov. 1788)

REIDENOUR, Nicholas, late of Balto., dec.; Thomas Rutter acting admnin. (BMJ, 24 Dec. 1790)

REITTEMAN, Christina Gertraut, midwife from Germany, informs the public that she reside in Howard's Street, next door to the southeast corner of Baltimore (Market) St. (BMJ, 27 Aug. 1790)

RETAKER, Adam, of Balto. Co., will not pay the debts of his wife Mary. (BMJ, 26 Sept. 1788)

RICE, Joseph, married Saturday last, Nancy, eldest daughter of John Gray of Baltimore. (BMJ, 19 Feb. 1788; BMG, 19 Feb. 1788)

RICE, Patrick, formerly of Phila., but resident in Baltimore for the past few years, died Saturday last. His remains were deposited in the Roman Catholic churchyard. (BMJ, 10 March 1789)

RICHARDSON, John, dec.; Frederick Pratt and Thorowgood Smith, admins. (BMG, 14 Feb. 1786)

RICHARDSON, Joseph, died at his seat in Dorchester Co., Tuesday, 2nd August, in his 43rd year, a magistrate and officer of militia. (BMJ, 11 Aug. 1786)

RICHARDSON, Thomas, of A. A. Co., will not pay the debts of his wife Hero. (AMG, 10 May 1787)

RIDDELL, Robert, of Baltimore, married on Sunday evening, by Rev. Dr. West, Miss Mary Hawksworth. (BMG, 14 March 1786)

RIDGATE, Thomas How, late of Port Tobacco, Chas. Co.; Elizabeth Ridgate, admnx. (AMG, 1 July 1790) John Forbes, attorney for the admnx. (BMJ, 6 Aug. 1790)

RIDGE, Jonathan, of Balto., and his wife Eleanor, have parted by mutual consent. (BMᵀ, 18 Sept. 1787)

RIDGELY, Charles, died Sunday, 17th inst., at his home in Balto. (BMG, 19 Dec. 1786)

RIDGELY, Charles, son of John, late of Balto. Co., dec.; John Risgely and Rebecca Ridgely, execs. (BMJ, 16 Feb. 1787)

RIDGELY, Capt. Charles, of Balto. Co., died yesterday morning in his 58th year. For the last 18 years he represented the county in the state legislature. (BMJ, 29 June 1790)

RIDGELY, HENRY, Esq., married in Balto., Miss Chase, daughter of the Hon. Samuel Chase. (BMJ, 12 June 1787) Bride's name is Matilda Chase, dau. of Samuel Chase. (BMG, 12 June 1787)

RIDGELY, Joshua, late of A. A. Co., dec.; Elizabeth Yieldhall, extx. (AMG, 28 June 1787)

RIDGELY, Mrs. Mary, died 21st inst., in her 61st year, relict of the late John Ridgely. (BMJ, 28 Feb. 1786)

RIDGELY, Mrs. Mary, died 21st inst., in her 61st year, relict of the late John Ridgely. (BMJ, 28 Feb. 1786)

RIDLEY, Matthew, merchant of Balto., married a few days ago at the seat of His Excellency Governor Livingston, near Elizabeth-Town, N. J., Catherine Livingston, daughter of the Governor. (BMJ, 1 May 1787)

RIDLEY, Matthew, died Friday last, aged 43 years. His remains were deposited in St. Paul's Churchyard. (BMJ, 17 Nov. 1789) Catherine Ridley, admnx. (BMG, 25 Dec. 1789)

RIGGEN, Jonathan, late of Worcester Co., dec.; his creditors will petition the Assembly to make sale of his real estate. (AMG, 26 Jan. 1786)

RIGGS, Elisha, of A. A. Co., dec.; Hamutal Welsh will settle the estate. (BMG, 20 Feb. 1787)

RIGGS, Ninian, of A. A. Co., dec.; T. Bicknell, admin. (AMG, 10 Dec. 1789)

RILEY, Barney, late of Harford Co., dec.; Jane Foster, extx., will petition the assembly for an act to make his will valid. (BMJ, 7 Sept. 1787)

NEWSPAPER GLEANINGS, 1786 - 1790

RISTEAU, Abraham, late of Balto. Co., dec.; Thomas Cradock, exec. (BMJ, 18 Sept. 1789)

RISTEAU, George, Jr., died Thursday last at his seat about nine miles from Balto., in his 26th year, leaving an infant daughter. (BMG, 17 March 1789) William Lux, exec. (BMJ, 1 Sept. 1789)

ROBERTS, John, sometime since of Annap., dec.; George Leigh, admin. (AMG, 19 April 1787)

ROBERTS, Levi, of Balto. Co., will not pay the debts of his wife Elizabeth who has behaved herself in a manner unbecoming the marriage state...has deserted him (list of other offenses given). (BMJ, 4 July 1786)

ROBERTSON, Capt. George, of Fells Point, dec.; Rosanna Robertson, admnx. (BMJ, 22 Dec. 1786)

ROBERTSON, James, Jr., wagonmaker, native of Currie, shire of Edinburgh, who lived for some time at Fells Point, where he had a wife and four children, three of whom were James and Ann and Elizabeth, should apply to Alexander Finlater, or to the printer, so he will have an opportunity to see his father who has just arrived here. (BMJ, 18 Aug. 1786)

ROBINSON, Alexander, merchant of Balto., married Thursday, 8th inst., at Walnut Grove in Frederick Co., Va., to Mrs. Priscilla Booth. (BMJ, 17 June 1788)

ROBINSON, George, late of Fells Point, dec.; George Hall and Elizabeth Hall, admins. (BMJ, 31 March 1789)

ROBINSON, James, late overseer of the A. A. Co. poor house, dec.; Richard Owen, James Robinson, execs. (AMG, 17 Jan. 1788)

ROBINSON, Mrs. Priscilla, wife of Alexander Robinson, merchant of Baltimore, died 7th inst., at Walnut Grove, Fred. Co., Va. (BMJ, 23 July 1790)

ROGERS, Charles, native of Ireland, lately arrived in Balto., will teach school. (BMJ, 3 Jan. 1786)

ROGERS, Mrs. Henrietta, died Wednesday last in her 62nd year. Funeral from Mr. Philip Rogers' in South Street. (BMJ, 28 May 1790)

ROGERS, Hon. John, Chancellor of the State of Md., died Wednesday last. (BMG, 29 Sept. 1789) Margaret Lee Rogers, admnx. (AMG, 22 Oct. 1789)

ROSS, Miss Prudence, died Tuesday, 7th inst., at Col. John Stull's, near Hegers Town, eldest daughter of the late Mrs. Stull, in her 21st year. (BMJ, 14 Aug. 1787)

ROSS, Richard, of Bladensburg, married Wednesday evening last in Balto.; Mrs. Sarah Brereton of Balto. (BMG, 6 Nov. 1789)

ROURKE, James, will not be responsible for the debts of his wife Sophia. (AMG, 6 Aug. 1789)

RUDULPH, Tobias, late of Head of Elk, Cecil Co.; Tobias Rudulph, exec. (BMJ, 6 Nov. 1787)

RUSSELL, James, died 1 Aug. at his house in Westminster, Eng., at an advanced age. In his earlier years he cultivated an extensive commerce with Va. and Md. (BMJ, 14 Nov. 1788)

RUSSELL, Josiah, late of Fred. Co., dec.; also Mary Russell, late of Fred. Co., dec.; A. Faw, admin. de bonis non. (BMJ, 30 July 1790)

RUSSELL, Thomas, of North East, dec.; Anne Russell, extx. (BMJ, 6 June 1786)

RUSSELL, Thomas, died Monday, 6th inst., in his 38th year. On Tuesday his remains were deposited in St. Paul's Burying Ground. Brethren of the several Free Mason Lodges paid their last tribute to a worthy brother. (BMG, 10 July 1789)

RUTLAND, Thomas, late of A. A. Co., dec.; W. Goldsmith, B. Whetcroft, trustees, will sell his valuable farm containing 1000 acres lying near Annapolis. (AMG, 4 March 1790)

RUTLAND, Thomas, son of Edmund, dec.; Gabriel Duvall, admin. (AMG, 23 Sept. 1790) The deceased kept stores at Oxford and Kingston. (EMH, 21 Sept. 1790)

RUTTER, Capt. Solomon, married Thursday last, Peggy Reitenauer, daughter of Nicholas Reitenauer. (BMJ, 16 Dec. 1788)

RUTTER, Thomas, Jr., married Saturday evening last, Polly Graybill, youngest daughter of Philip Graybill of Baltimore. (BMG, 20 Nov. 1787)

RYAN, Edward, butcher, drowned Friday last, when he fell out of a boat into Jones Falls. He leaves a wife and five small children. (BMJ, 10 Oct. 1786)

SAMPSON, Richard; his sons Richard and Isaac warn anyone from buying two tracts of land "Harding's Adventure," and "Sampson's Addition,"whereon Richard Role now   lives, on the south side of Back River. (BMG, 4 Sept. 1789)

SANDERS, Mrs. Anne, dec.; Frederick Green, exec. (AMG, 29 Oct. 1789)

SANDERS, Joshua, of Chas. Co., dec.; Ann Sanders, extx. (BMG, 3 Jan. 1786)

SCHLEY, John Thomas, died Wed., 24th inst., in Frederick Town, in his 79th year. He was one of the earliest settlers in this place, and in the year 1746 when Frederick Town was laid out, built the   first house on it. "Frederick, 27 Nov." (BMJ, 7 Dec. 1790)

SCOTT, Andrew, has removed goods from his house and will not be responsible for the debts of his wife Priscilla. (BMJ, 22 June 1787) Priscill Scott, formerly Colvin, refutes her husband's charges. (BMJ, 26 June 1787)

SCOTT, George, of A. A. Co., dec.; Hellen Scott, admnx. (BMJ, 20 Oct. 1789)

SCOTT, John, Esq., attorney at law, lately married Betsy Goodwin Dorsey of Balto. Co. (BMG, 23 May 1788)

SEARS, Mrs. Jane, wife of Samuel Sears, a major in the service of the British East India Co., died Saturday last at the house of her brother Matthew Ridley, in her 32nd year. Her remains were deposited last evening in St. Paul's Churchyard. (BMJ, 17 April 1787)

SELBY, Benjamin, late of A. A. Co., dec.; Joseph Selby, admin. (AMG, 13 Sept. 1787)

SELMAN, Mrs. Sarah, consort of Johnzee Selman of Balto., died Wednesday last, aged 27 years. (BMJ, 12 March 1790)

SEMMES, Thomas, of Chas. Co.; his sons James, Edward, and Joseph Milburn Semmes, intend to petition the Assembly for an act to appoint trustees for selling "Hall's Lot," 130 a., in order to pay a debt owing from their father to a certain Joseph Semmes, formerly of Md., but now of Liege, Europe. (AMG, 15 March 1787)

SENEY, Hon. Joshua, of Md., married Saturday evening last at New York by Rev. Dr. Lynn, Fanny Nicholson, daughter of James Nicholson, of that city. (BMJ, 11 May 1790)

SEWELL, William, will not pay the debts of his wife Mary Ann. (BMJ, 29 Aug. 1786)

SHEKELL, John, late of A. A. Co., dec.; Abraham Sgekell, Francis Shekell, and Benjamin Basford, execs. (AMG, 29 Nov. 1787)

SHEPHERD, Mrs. Ann, died Sunday last, in her 86th year, at the house of her son Peter Shepherd, Esq., of this town, relict of Mr. Adam Shepherd, of Bucks Co., Penna., who paid the great debt of nature about half a century ago. (BMJ, 13 Jan. 1786)

SHEPHERD, Mary, daughter of Peter Shepherd of Baltimore Town, Esq., died last Friday night, aged about 16 years. (BMJ, 27 Feb. 1787) Her remains were interred in the German Evangelical Reformed Church Burying Ground. (BMG, 27 Feb. 1787)

SHEPHERD, Peter, died yesterday morning at an advanced age...whose probity and patriotism justly gained him the confidence and support of his countrymen, having repeatedly been honoured with a seat in the General Assembies of Penna. and Md. (BMJ, 13 Nov. 1787)

SHIPLEY, Talbot, trustee, advertises the sale of lands belonging to his father, George Shipley. The notice gives the location and a description of the land. (BMG, 19 May 1786)

SHRAKES, Tedrick, of Balto., will not pay the debts of his wife Margaret. (BMJ, 31 July 1787)

SHUMAN, Peter, late of Frederick Co., dec.; Michael Troutman, exec. (FMC, 20 Sept. 1786)

SIMMONS, Knighton, late of A. A. Co., dec.; John Simmons, admin. (AMG, 4 Dec. 1788)

SIMPSON, James, late of Charles Co., dec.; Catherine Simpson, Thomas Simpson, admins. (AMG, 24 Dec. 1789)

SIMPSON, James, merchant of Baltimore, married Thursday evening, 21st inst., at Mt. Serenity, Lancaster Co., Penna., Miss Clingan, daughter of the late James Clingan. (BMJ, 29 Jan. 1790)

SIMPSON, William, late of A. A. Co., dec.; Thomas Cook, exec. (BMJ, 23 Jan. 1787)

SKINNER, Capt. Thomas, late of New York, married Tuesday evening last, Betsey Crockett of Baltimore. (BMJ, 6 Oct. 1786)

SLADE, William, advertises that his house, known as Slade's Tavern, and the adjoining 223 and 3/4 acres of land, on the main road leading from Baltimore to Little York and Lancaster, 22 miles from Baltimore, and 34 from Lancaster, will be sold. (YPH, 26 May 1790)

SMITH, ---, a son of Col. Samuel Smith, died Saturday when a pottery coop fell on him; aged four years. (Correction: a poultry coop) (BMJ, 18 Nov. 1788)

SMITH, Charles, of Chas. Co., dec.; Mary Smith, extx. (AMG, 11 Feb. 1790)

SMITH, Francis, died in this town. (BMJ, 15 Sept. 1789) Francis Smith, Sr., late of Baltimore, dec.; Alice Smith, adminx. (BMG, 27 Oct. 1789)

SMITH, George, of Baltimore, died lately on the schooner Betty, Capt. Wallace, on her passage from Surinam to Boston. (BMJ, 13 Aug. 1790)

SMITH, James, an assistant in Gibson's office, drowned Sunday afternoon. (BMG, 22 May 1787)

SMITH, James, merchant, died yesterday in his 35th year, eldest son of William Smith, Esq., (BMJ, 15 April 1788)

SMITH, Mordecai, of Calvert Co., dec.; George Smith and Phebe Smith, admins. (AMG, 16 March 1786)

SMITH, Col. Richard, died Saturday morning last in this town (Frederick). His remains were interred on the Sunday following in the English burying ground. (FMC, 14 March 1787)

SMITH, Robert, Esq., and Peggy, daughter of the Hon. William Smith of Baltimore, were married by Rev. Dr. Allison on Tuesday last. (BMJ, 10 Dec. 1790)

SMITH, Rowland, late of Balto., dec.; George Welch, surviving executor. (BMG, 21 April 1786)

SMITH, Thomas, of Baltimore, will not pay the debts of his wife Mary. (BMJ, 15 Oct. 1790)

SMOCK, John, moved to N. C. about three years ago, leaving his children in the care of the subscriber, James Wilson, of Wor. Co. (AMG, 3 Jan. 1788)

SNELL, George, dec.; Helen Scott, adminx. (AMG, 21 May 1789)

SOLLERS, Heighe, late of Balto. Co., dec.; Jehu Bowen and Jeremiah Johnson, Jr., execs. (BMJ, 8 Dec. 1786)

SOLLERS, Sabrett, died Thursday last, at his seat on Patapsco Neck. (BMJ, 1 Aug. 1786) J. Walters, exec. (BMJ, 2 Jan. 1787)

SOMERVELL, James, of Baltimore, and Nancy Ralph were married. (BMJ, 30 Jan. 1787)

SOMERVELL, Mr. John, late of St. M. Co., dec.; George Clarke Somervell, exec. (AMG, 28 May 1789)

SOMERVILLE, Mrs. Margaret, of St. M. Co., dec.; John De Butts, exec. ((AMG, 16 Feb. 1786)

SPEAR, William, merchant, died yesterday morning, in his 68th year. Long obit is given. (BMJ, 29 Dec. 1789) Samuel Smith, William Patterson, admins. (BMG, 19 Jan. 1790)

SPECK, John, skinner, was crushed to death when he was thrown under the wagon he was riding on Thursday last. About 18 years ago his brother lost his life in a similar accident. (BMJ, 30 Sept. 1788) Mary Ann Speck, adminx. (BMJ, 9 June 1789)

SPENCER, Isaac, dec.; left a son and heir, Isaac Spencer. The notice is signed by Hannah Spencer amd Benjamin Roberts. (AMG, 14 Sept. 1786)

SPRIGG, Edward, late of P. G. Co., dec.; R'd Sprigg, Jr., admin. (AMG, 13 May 1790)

SPRIGG, Dr. John, of P. G. Co., dec.; Richard Sprigg, admin. (AMG, 4 Oct. 1787)

SPRY, Rev. Francis, died last Saturday morning in his 28th year, late of Tal. Co., a truly evangelical preacher of the Methodist Society. On Sunday morning his remains were deposited in the Methodist burying ground. The sermon was delivered by Rev. Mr. Cooper. (BMJ, 26 May 1789)

STANSBURY, Emanuel, died Sunday last, at Fells Point, in his 54th year. His remains will be interred in the family burying ground, near Curtis Creek, A. A. Co. (BMJ, 30 Nov. 1790)

STANSBURY, Luke, late of Back River Neck, Balto. Co., dec.; Catherine Stansbury and Daniel Stansbury, admins. (BMG, 12 Sept. 1786) The admins. warn all persons not to take an assignment of a bond that passed about 25 Jan. 1785 from Stansbury to Cornelius Wells for two cords of firewood. (BMJ, 3 Aug. 1787)

STAYTON, Jacob, late of Dor. Co., dec.; Richard Stanford, admin. (AMG, 18 March 1790)

STAYTON, Sally, eldest daughter of William Stayton, merchant of Balto., died last Saturday. (BMJ, 9 Nov. 1787)

STEEL, James, printer, died Tuesday, 15th Aug., in Philadelphia, in his 23rd year. His remains were decently interred in the Presbyterian Burial Ground. (FMC, 20 Sept. 1786)

STEEMER, Anthony, Jr., died a few days ago at Lancaster, Pa., in his 24th year, a printer. (BMJ, 25 April 1788)

STEIDINGER, Frederick, died Saturday morning last, in his 64th year, one of the old inhabitants of Elizabeth Town. On Sunday his remains were interred in the High German Lutheran Burial Ground. (EWS, 30 Dec. 1790)

STEITZ, Michael, of Balto. Town, dec.; Mary Steitz, Christian Deal, Philip Highjoe, execs. (BMJ, 10 July 1789)

STERETT, George, lately died on his passage to England, son of Mr. James Sterett of Baltimore. (BMJ, 4 April 1786)

STERETT, John, merchant of Baltimore, died and was interred in the Presbyterian Churchyard. (BMG, 2 Jan. 1787) James Sterett, Deborah Sterett, and Samuel Sterett, execs. (BMG, 30 Jan. 1787)

STERETT, Samuel, Esq., of Baltimore, and Rebecca, daughter of the late Col. Isaac Sears of New York, were married Thursday, 20th inst., at New York by the Right Rev. Bishop Provost. (BMJ, 1 June 1790)

STEVENS, Dennis, of A. A. Co., dec.; Vachel Stevens, exec. (AMG, 31 Aug. 1786)

STEVENS, Vachel, late of A. A. Co., dec.; Zachariah Jacob, admin. (AMG, 24 July 1788)

STEVENSON, Dr. John, late of Baltimore Town, dec.; John Stevenson and William Hammond, the execs., advertise the sale of a 168 acre tract in Frederick Co. call "Bare Hills." (BMG, 6 March 1787)

STEWART, Mrs., wife of Major William Stewart, died at Marshall Hall, Md. (BMJ, 19 May 1789)

STEWART, Anthony, former resident of Annapolis, now of Nova Scotia. R. Denny and Ben. Latimer are trustees to settle his affairs. (AMG, 2 April 1789)

STEWART, James, died leaving a widow Elizabeth. (AMG, 27 July 1786)

STEYER, George, merchant of Baltimore, died Saturday, 10th inst. He was buried in the Evangelical Reformed Burying Ground on Howard's Hill. (BMJ, 16 June 1786) Nancy Steyer, William Baker, John Hagerty, Jr., execs. (BMG, 18 July 1786)

STEYER, Nancy, of Baltimore, intends to petition the assembly for an act enabling her to dispose of certain property in Baltimore Town, willed to her by her husband George Steyer. (BMJ, 1 April 1788)

STOCKETT, Lewis, of A. A. Co., dec.; Anne Stockett, extx. (AMG, 12 Jan. 1786)

STONE, Mrs. Margaret, wife of the Hon. Thomas Stone, departed this life, 1st June. (AMG, 7 June 1787)

STONE, Thomas, late of Annap., dec.; M. J. Stone, and G. R. Brown, execs. (AMG, 10 Jan. 1788)

STORY, Ralph, late of Balto., dec.; Elizabeth Young, John Young, execs. (BMJ, 20 Feb. 1789; BMJ, 27 April 1790)

STRAN, Capt. John, and Rebecca Johnson, daughter of William Johnson, sailmaker, of Fells Point, were married Thursday evening last. (BMG, 5 Oct. 1790)

STRICKLAND, John, left England in 1775 and arrived in Baltimore. He should apply to Capt. William Dennis of the ship Hanbury, or to John Clapham, of Annap. (AMG, 5 July 1787) Strickland, of the parish of Camberwell, Surrey, near London, who came from England under indenture from late Messrs. Lux and Bowly in 1775, to serve as a gardner, should apply to the printer. (BMJ, 23 July 1790)

STRICKSTROKE, Adam, of Frederick Town, will not pay the debts of his wife, Otillow. (FMC, 28 Nov. 1787)

STULL, John, dec.; C. Beall advertises for debtors and creditors to settle their accounts. (EWS, 7 Dec. 1790)

STULL, Mrs. Mercy, wife of Capt. John Stull of Washington Co., and sister of Gen. Williams of Baltimore, died Tuesday last. (BMJ, 13 Feb. 1787.)

SUIT, Jesse B., will not pay the debts of his wife Sarah. (AMG, 9 Aug. 1787)

SULLIVAN, Cornelius, left Dublin about 5 years ago and landed in Baltimore. If living he should contact his son Philip living in York Co., Penna. (BMG, 17 Nov. 1789) He left Dublin, Ireland, about 6 years ago in company with a Mr. Martin, a surgeon, and landed at Baltimore. Sullivan's son Philip would be glad to hear from him. Letters should be directed to Robert McIlheney at Peter Little's Town, York Co. (YPH, 7 April 1790)

SUMMERS, Jacob, drowned attempting to cross Stigar's Run last Saturday evening. (BMJ, 11 Aug. 1789)

SUMMERS, John, a native of Md., died in Va. in his 103rd year. In 1715 he settled in Alexandria Co., Va. He leaves grandchildren, great-grandchildren, and great-great-grandchildren. (BMG, 31 Dec. 1790)

SWAN, Major John, of Balto., and Eliza Maxwell of Myrtle Grove, Talbot Co., were married at the latter place on 12th inst. (BMJ, 17 July 1787)

SWAN, Joseph, merchant, and Nancy Maxwell, were married last evening. (BMJ, 8 Oct. 1790)

TAGART, John, merchant of Baltimore, and Polly Williamson of Balto. Co., were married Tuesday last. (BMJ, 15 Oct. 1790)

TALBOT, Benjamin R., of Baltimore Co., dec.; Martha Talbot, extx. (BMJ, 20 Feb. 1789)

TANEY, Michael, dec.; Frederick Crisman, Sr., Conrad Orndorf, execs. (BMJ, 19 Sept. 1788)

TATLOW, Joseph, of Baltimore, will not be responsible for the debts of his wife Mary. (BMJ, 4 Jan. 1788)

THOMAS, George, of St. M. Co., dec.; William Thomas, Jr., admin. (AMG, 17 Sept. 1789)

THOMAS, Richard, of Cecil Co., dec.; his land will be sold by Richard S. Thomas. (BMJ, 3 Nov. 1786)

THOMAS, William, and his two children were murdered by savages on 25th April last, on the headwaters of Dunkard Creek, Washington Co. (BMJ, 26 May 1789)

THOMPSON, Andrew, late of Baltimore Town, Agnes Thompson, admnx. (BMJ, 28 Nov. 1786)

THOMPSON, Col. John D., of Cecil Co., dec.; James Louttit, W. Matthews, execs.
    (AMG, 13 Dec. 1787)

THORN, Susannah, of Bladensburg, dec.; Robert Wade, admin. (AMG, 19 Feb. 1789)

TIERNEY, William, son of Michael Tierny, formerly of Limerick, Ireland, c.1777,
    left that city and embarked at Cork for North America, and is supposed to
    have been at Phila. or New York in 1786. (BMJ, 15 Jan. 1790)

TILGHMAN, Matthew, Esq., died suddenly 4th inst., at his seat in Talbot Co.,
    in his 73rd year. (BMJ, 18 May 1790)

TILGHMAN, Tench, died Tuesday afternoon at his house in Baltimore, merchant;
    when he acted as officer in the American army he was honored by the friend-
    ship of our illustrious commander in chief. (BMG, 21 April 1786)

TILGHMAN, Thomas Ringgold, partner of James Carey, died. (BMJ, 4 May 1790)

TOFT, Thomas, lived near Governor's Bridge, dec.; Samuel Jacob, admin. de bonis
    non. (AMG, 5 Oct. 1786)

TOOLE, Mrs. Hetty, wife of James Toole of Baltimore, died yesterday in her 27th
    year. (BMJ, 8 Jan. 1788)

TOOLE, James, merchant, and Mrs. Hetty Noble, were married. (BMJ, 19 Dec. 1786)

TOOLE, James, merchant, of Baltimore, and Mrs. Susannah Moore, were married
    Saturday evening last. (BMJ, 12 Aug. 1788)

TOOTELL, James, of Annapolis, dec.; Anne Tootell, extx. (AMG, 23 March 1786)
    James Williams and Joseph Dowson, acting admins. (AMG, 27 April 1786)

TOWNSEND, Henry, and Rebecca Chesley, third daughter of John Chesley, Esq., of
    of St. M. Co., were married 11th ult., at Hayes, Montgomery Co. (BMG, 6
    Jan. 1786)

TOWNSEND, Joseph, and Polly, daughter of George Matthews, were married yester-
    day at Friends Meeting. (BMJ, 1 June 1787)

TOWSON, Jacob, and Jane Boyd, were married last Saturday evening. (BMJ, 22
    April 1788)

TRAVERSE, Henry, of Dor. Co., will petition the assembly to aid in the execution
    of the last will and testament of his father, John Hicks Traverse, of Dor.
    Co., dec. (BMJ, 19 Sept. 1788)

TREWELL, or TROWELL, William, native of England, who in April, 1780, lived in
    some part of Md., and was finally with a Dr. Bate of Georgetown, should
    apply to Richard Curson of Baltimore. (BMJ, 27 March 1787)

TROUP, Dr. John, died Friday evening last, in this town. He leaves a wife and children. The next day his remains were interred in St. Pauls Churchyard. (BMJ, 22 May 1787) Christopher Johnston, admin. (BMJ, 3 July 1787)

TROWEL, William, native of Berbyshire, of Great Britain; late resident of Md., should apply to the printer, or to Edward Ingleton, of Lower Ferry, Trenton, Penna. (BMJ, 5 Aug. 1788)

TROXELL, Abraham, dec.; John Hager, exec. (EWS, 14 Oct. 1790)

TRUMBO, John, of Balto., will pay no debts of his wife Catherine. (BMJ, 27 July 1790)

TSCHUDY, Winbert, of Balto. Town, dec.; Elizabeth and Martin Tschudy, admins. (BMG, 7 Nov. 1786)

TUCKER, Mrs., consort of St. George Tucker, died a few days ago in Chesterfield Co., Va. (BMJ, 12 Feb. 1788)

TUKE, Miss Sarah, member of the American Company of Comedians, died at Chester on her way to Baltimore. (BMJ, 11 Sept. 1787)

TUNSTILL, Henry, late of Baltimore, dec.; William Tinker, Caleb Hewitt, execs. (BMJ, 30 Nov. 1790)

TURNBULL, Robert, of Petersburg, Va., and Mrs. Sarah Buchanan, were married on Monday last at the seat of John Robert Holliday in Baltimore Co.. (BMJ, 19 March 1790)

TURNER, Edward, dec.; Joseph Queen of Bladensburg, exec. (BMJ, 1 Sept. 1789)

TYLER, Dr. John, and Catharina Harrison, both or Frederick-Town, were married there on 19th inst. (BMJ, 27 April 1787)

TYLER, Mrs. Susanna, wife of Samuel Tyler, died at her husband's seat on Patuxent, in P. G. Co. (BMJ, 2 May 1788)

TYSON, Jesse, of Harford Co., and Peggy, daughter of the late John Hopkins, dec., were married 1st inst. at Indian Spring Friends Meeting. (BMJ, 9 April 1790)

USHER, Anne, died Monday evening last in her 19th year, eldest daughter of Mf. Thomas Usher, late of Baltimore Town. Her remains were deposited Wednesday evening in St. Paul's Churchyard. (BMJ, 11 Sept. 1789)

USHER, James, of Baltimore, merchant, died Thursday last in his 20th year. He was buried in St. Paul's Churchyard. (BMJ, 1 July 1788) He was a son of the late Thomas Usher, merchant, and died 26th ult., in his 18th year. (BMG, 1 July 1788)

USHER, Mr. Thomas, died Tuesday evening last, merchant, in his 49th year. His remains will be interred this day in St. Paul's Churchyard; he was an affectionate husband and parent. (BMJ, 27 Jan. 1786) Thomas Usher, Joseph Usher, Samuel Johnson, Joseph Donaldson, execs. (BMJ, 3 March 1786)

VALENTINE, John, of Norfolk, dec.; Anne Valentine, adminx. (BMJ, 11 July 1786)

VAN BIBBER, Andrew, and Sally, daughter of Ezekiel Forman, Esq., were married a few days ago at Chester Town, Kent Co. (BMJ, 26 Feb. 1790)

VAN BIBBER, Mrs. Elizabeth, consort of James Van Bibber, of Baltimore, merchant, and daughter of Edward Dorsey, died Thursday last, in her 24th year, at the seat of her brother Edward Dorsey. (BMJ, 16 Feb. 1790)

VAN BIBBER, James, merchant, and Betsey, daughter of Edward Dorsey, were married. (BMJ, 27 Feb. 1787)

VAN DYCK, Henry, died in Albany. (BMJ, 10 Feb. 1786)

VEAZEY, William, of Cecil Co., will not pay the debts of his wife Sarah. (BMJ, 3 April 1787)

WADDRINGTON, Dr., of Georgetown, Md., and Betsy Booth, were married lately in Williamsburg. (BMG, 29 Feb. 1788)

WAGGAMAN, John Martin, late of Balto., dec.; John Leypold, admin. (BMJ, 26 June 1789)

WAILES, Benjamin, late of P. G. Co., dec.; Levin Covington Wailes and Susannah Wailes, admins. (AMG, 22 Oct. 1789)

WALLACE, Mrs. Eleanor, wife of Dr. Michael Wallace, died 26th inst. at her father's residence, near Nottingham, Patuxent. (BMJ, 7 Aug. 1787)

WALLER, Benjamin, died at Williamsburg, in his 70th year. (BMJ, 16 May 1786)

WALKER, Capt. Thomas, late of A. A. Co., dec.; Nicholas Watkins, admin. (AMG, 15 June 1786)

WALTERS, Samuel W., late of Balto. Co., dec.; Eleanor Walters, adminx. (BMJ, 6 Oct. 1786)

WARD, Edward, late of Middle River Neck, Balto. Co.; George Franciscus a guardian. (BMJ, 1 Sept. 1786)

WARFIELD, Azel, late of A. A. Co., dec.; Charles Alexander Warfield, admin. (BMJ, 3 Jan. 1786)

WARFIELD, Col. Charles, late of Fred. Co., dec.; Elizabeth Warfield and Alexander Warfield, admins. (BMJ, 8 Oct. 1790)

WARFIELD, Joseph, late of A. A. Co., dec.; Richard W. Turner, admin. (AMG, 30 April 1789)

WARFIELD, Luke, of A. A. Co., dec.; John Warfield, admin. (AMG, 10 Dec. 1789)

WARREN, John, a native of Talbot Co., aged 19, escaped from A. A. Co. jail. (AMG, 31 Aug. 1786)

WASKEY, Christian, intending to move into the country will sell his house and lot in Queen St., Fells Point. (BMJ, 14 March 1786)

WATERS, Jacob, late of Mont. Co., dec.; Elizabeth Waters, extx. (AMG, 14 June 1787)

WATERS, Joseph, late of A. A. Co., dec.; Elizabeth Waters, extx. (AMG, 31 July 1788)

WATERS, Samuel Wright, died Thursday last, at his plantation in this county, in his 36th year. (BMJ, 29 Aug. 1786)

WATERS, William, late of Mont. Co., dec.; Zachariah Waters, exec. (BMJ, 17 Oct. 1788)

WATHEN, Elizabeth, will petition the assembly for a sum of money for maintenance for her son Ballekiah, who is insane. (AMG, 17 Jan. 1788)

WATKINS, Gassaway, security of Capt. Thomas Harwood, died, leaving a widow Dinah. (AMG, 10 Sept. 1789)

WATKINS, Joseph, late of A. A. Co., dec.; Anne Watkins, extx. (AMG, 16 April 1789)

WATKINS, Thomas, late of A. A. Co., dec.; Elizabeth Watkins, adminx. (AMG, 30 Nov. 1786)

WATKINS, Thomas, of P. G. Co., dec.; Col. John Addison and his wife are admins. (AMG, 2 Sept. 1790)

WAUGH, William, died Saturday last in his 56th year; a native of Scotland, he arrived here a few days ago from Jamaica. On Sunday his remains were deposited in the New Presbyterian Burying Ground. (BMJ, 18 Nov. 1788)

WAYART, Barbara, of Washington Co. will petition the assembly for a divorce from her husband Michael Wayart. (BMJ, 26 Oct. 1787)

WEADGE, Joseph, of Balto., will not pay the debts of his wife Mary, formerly Mary Juble: "Now, Devil, do you worst." (BMJ, 13 July 1790

WEAVER, Daniel, of Balto., will not be responsible for the debts of his wife Eve. (BMG, 9 July 1790)

WEBB, John, was executed near Baltimore, Wednesday last. (BMG, 13 Feb. 1789)

WEBSTER, Elizabeth, late of Balto., dec.; James and Joseph Bankson, execs. (BMG, 11 Nov. 1788)

WEEMS, Mrs. Alice, wife of Mr. John Weems, and daughter of the late President Le ., died at Weems' Forest, Cal. Co., on the 25th July. (BMG, 8 Sept. 1789)

WEEMS, John, Esq., late a resident of Delaware, and Alice, daughter of the Hon. Richard Lee, dec., were married a few days ago at Blenheim, Chas. Co. (BMJ, 1 April 1788)

WELLS, George, of Balto., dec.; George Wells and Lydia Wells, execs. (BMJ, 1 June 1787)

WELLS, George, Jr., of Fells Point, dec.; Hannah Wells, adminx. (BMJ, 10 April 1789)

WELSH, Edward, of Balto. Co., will not pay the debts of his wife Prudence, who has eloped. (BMJ, 15 Sept. 1789)

WELSH, John, late of Balto. Co., dec.; Thomas Sam. Pole, Elam Bailey, and John Geoghegan, admins. (BMJ, 22 Aug. 1786)

WELSH, Marcus, of Balto., will not pay the debts of his wife, Hannah, "who hath behaved herself in a dishonorable manner towards (me) and may from her natural depravity of mind," may seek to injure me further by running me in debt. (BMJ, 26 May 1786)

WELSH, Prudence, refutes the charges made by her husband, Edward. (BMJ, 25 Sept. 1789)

WELCH, Robert, of A. A. Co., dec.; Benjamin Welch and Robert Welch, execs. (AMG, 2 March 1786)

WEST, Stephen, and his wife advertise they will petition for restoration of a tract called "Black Acre" formerly the property of William Black, merchant of London, who the subscribers are heir to. (AMG, 3 Dec. 1789)

WEST, Stephen, Esq., late of P. G. Co.; dec., died Sunday morning last. (BMJ, 5 Jan. 1790)

NEWSPAPER GLEANINGS, 1786 - 1790

WEST, Mrs. Susannah, consort of Rev. Dr. William West, rector of St. Pauls
    Church, in Baltimore, died Friday evening last, aged 49 years. (BMJ, 17
    July 1787)

WHETSELL, Peter, late of Balto. Co., dec.; Isaac Day, John Whetsell, admins.
    (BMG, 15 Feb. 1788)

WHITAKER, Robert, late of P. G. Co., dec.; Margery Whitaker, adminx. (AMG, 16
    Dec. 1790)

WHITE, John, postmaster of Baltimore, died yesterday morning, in his 36th year,
    leaving a widow and five children. (BMJ, 21 May 1790)   D. Delozier, admin.
    (BMJ, 9 July 1790)

WHITE, Michael, age c. 13, son of Michael White, the blue dyer, has run away
    from Richardson Stuart. (BMJ, 20 Oct. 1789)

WHITER, John, late of Balto. Co., dec.; Isaac Henry, exec. (BMJ, 4 Aug. 1786)

WHITTINGTON, John Rousby, of Wor. Co., will petition the assembly to pass a law
    enabling him to make a will devised him by his late father William Whitting-
    ton. (BMJ, 18 March 1788). (Correction - enabling him mm to sell land
    devised him...)

WHITTINGTON, Thomas, late of A. A. Co., dec.; Thomas Whittington, exec. (AMG,
    12 Feb. 1789)

WHITTINGTON, William, of Wor. Co., died, leaving a will which devised property to
    his son John Rousby Whittington. (AMG, 17 April 1788)

WIESENTHAL, Dr. Andrew, of Baltimore, and Sally Van Dyke of Chester, were wed
    Tuesday last at Hilltop. (BMJ, 7 May 1790)

WIESENTHAL, Dr. Charles Frederick, died yesterday morning in his 63rd year, after
    having practiced physic in Baltimore for about 34 years. He leaves an only
    son. (BMJ, 2 June 1789) Elizabeth Wiesenthal, admnx. (BMJ, 19 June 1789)

WILCOXON, Anthony, dec.; Ruth Wilcoxon and Thomas Swearingen, execs. (BMG, 13
    Oct. 1789)

WILKINSON, William, dec.; his plantation in Patapsco Neck to be sold. /s/ Samuel
    Owings. (BMJ, 8 Sept. 1789)

WILLIAMS, Baruch, died Saturday, 20th ult., in Cecil Co. (BMJ, 16 March 1790)

WILLIAMS, John, of Fells Point, will not be responsible for the debts of his
    wife Hannah. (BMG, 7 Dec. 1790)

WILLIAMS, Joseph, of St. M. Co., dec.; left land to his sons William and James. Anne Williams, James Williams, and James Head will petition the assembly for an act to sell these lands. (AMG, 16 Sept. 1790)

WILLIAMS, Planner, dec.; John Gale, of Som. Co., exec. (BMG, 2 April 1790)

WILLIAMS, Mrs. Rachel, died 6th ult., at Elkton, Cecil Co., wife of Baruch Williams, clerk of the county. She was interred at St. Mary Ann's Parish Church. A funeral discourse was preached by Rev. Joseph Couden. (BMJ, 16 March 1790)

WILLIAMSON, Rev. Alexander, died Sunday, 19th ult., at Hayes. (BMG, 5 Dec. 1786) Henry Townsend, Benjamin Stoddert, Thomas Johns, execs. (BMJ, 5 Oct. 1787)

WILLIAMSON, Daniel, died Wednesday morning last in his 28th year. His remains were interred in St. Paul's Churchyard. (BMJ, 11 July 1788)

WILLIAMSON, Thomas, late of Balto. Co., dec.; Samuel Williamson, exec. (BMJ, 16 Oct. 1789)

WILSON, Benjamin, of Harf. Co., and Betsey, daughter of William Worthington of Baltimore County, were married Thursday last. (BMJ, 15 Aug. 1786)

WILSON, Stephen, of Baltimore, and Miss Rebecca Neilson, of Fells Point, were married a few days ago. (BMG, 21 Feb. 1786)

WILSON, Thomas, of Baltimore Co., will not pay the debts of his wife Ann. (BMJ, 29 June 1790)

WINCHESTER, William, Sr., died Friday evening last in Fred. Co., in his 80th year; a native of England. (BMG, 10 Sept. 1790)

WINGARD, John, of George-Town, dec.; Anthony Goszler is empowered by the exec. to settle accounts. (BMJ, 4 July 1788)

WINNING, Capt. John, of Balto., died Friday night last, in his 48th year. On Saturday his remains were interred in the new Presbyterian Burying Ground. (Bmg, 14 July 1789). Margaret Winning, adminx. (BMJ, 4 Aug. 1789)

WINSHIP, Mrs. Anne, died at Martinsburg, Berkeley Co., Va., on 26th inst., wife of Winn Winship, merchant of that place. (BMJ, 4 Sept. 1789)

WINSHIP, Iwinn of Talbot Co., will petition the assembly to annul jis marriage to his wife Maria. (AMG, 20 Dec. 1787)

WINTHROP, Thomas Lindal, and Miss Temple, daughter of the Hon. John Temple, Esq., H. B. M. Consul-General residing in this city, were married 25th ult., in Boston. (BMG, 15 Aug. 1786)

WIRT, William, a minor, will petition the assembly for a law to enable him to
sell his patrimony to enable him to complete his studies; also to sell
a moiety in a house and lot willed to his brother Jacob. (BMJ, 12 Sept.
1788)

WISE, Barbara, late of Balto. Town, dec.; Christian Keener, admin. (BMG, 10
Jan. 1786)

WOLFE, George, of Frederick Co., son of Peter Wolfe, dec. (BMG, 19 Oct. 1787)

WOOD, Robert, late of Baltimore Co.; his widow Jane, now Jane Cassidy, will
petition the assembly. (BMJ, 12 Sept. 1786)

WOOD, Zebedee, late of A. A. Co., dec.; Jerningham Drury will settle the estate.
(AMG, 17 April 1788)

WOOLSEY, John, late of Port-a-Down in the Kingdom of Ireland, dec.; walter Roe,
admin. (BMG, 19 May 1789)

WOOTTON, Singleton, merchant of Queen Anne Town, Patuxent, died 1st inst., after
a tedious illness. (BMG, 6 Nov. 1788) Richard Wootton, exec. (BMJ, 20
Jan. 1789)

WORKMAN, Hugh, boatwright, late of Baltimore Town, dec.; Thomas Pilkingon ,
Mary Workman, and Elizabeth Workman, execs. (BMJ, 14 Feb. 1786)

WORRELL, Edward, died lately in Kent Co., High Sheriff of that county. He is
succeeded by Josiah Johnson. (BMJ, 8 Jan. 1790)

WORTHINGTON, Charles, late of A. A. Co., dec.; John, Samuel, and Thomas Worthington, execs. (BMG, 6 Jan. 1786)

WORTHINGTON, William, of Balto. Co., will not pay the debts of his wife Elizabeth. (BMJ, 20 Jan. 1789)

WRIGHT, John; his son Turbutt Wright, a minor, was conveyed "Smith's First
Choice," by William Schoolfield. (AMG, 19 Nov. 1789)

WRIGHT, Thomas, late of A. A. Co., dec.; Philip Hammond, admin. (AMG, 1 March
1787)

YARNELL, Mr. Uriah, of this place, died Saturday night, aged about 30. He
was interred in Friends Burial Ground. (EMH, 17 Aug. 1790) Martha Hall,
adminx. (EMH, 28 Dec. 1790)

YEALDHALL, William, late of A. A. Co., dec.; Samuel Yealdhall, exec. (AMG,
11 March 1790)

YEDDELL, William, late of A. A. Co., dec.; John Jarvis, admin. de bonis non. (AMG, 4 Nov. 1790)

YOUNG, Mrs. Margaret, died 25th ult., at Hagerstown, Washington Co., in her 36th year, consort of George Young, minister of the German Lutheran Church of that town. (BMJ, 9 Oct. 1789)

YOUNG, Samuel, late of Baltimore, dec.; Rebecca Young, extx. (BMJ, 31 Aug. 1787)

YOUNG, William, died Tuesday evening last at "Chatsworth," the seat of George Lux; merchant of Baltimore in his 50th year. He was buried last evening in St. Paul's Churchyard. (BMJ, 25 July 1788) Arabella Young, extx. (BMJ, 29 July 1788)

ZACHARIE, Stephen, French merchant, and Ann Waters, dau. of Philip Waters, merchant who lately arrived here from Holland, were married last Saturday evening. (BMJ, 15 May 1787)

ZIMMER, Mr.; died (date not given). (FMC, 6 Dec. 1786)

ADDENDA

BROTHERSON, Charles, and Jane Stansbury, were married last evening at Fells Point. (BMG, 23 July 1790)

INDEX

ADAMS, William, 36
ADDISON, Col. John, 61
ALCOCK, James, 4
ALKINS, Polly, 23
ALLISON, Rev. Dr., 54
ANGELL, Brig.-Gen., 23
    Abigail, 23
ASHMAN, George, 43
ASKEW, Wm., 27

BAILEY, Elam, 62
BAKER, William, 56
BALLARD, Robert, 46
BANKSON, James, 62
    Joseph, 62
BARNEY, Polly, 3
BASEMAN, John, 44
BASFORD, Benjamin, 52
BAYER, Michael, 25
BAYLY, M., 19
BEAL, Eunice, 3
BEALL, C., 56
    John, 39
BEARD, Richard, Jr., 41
BEASMAN, John, 44
BICKNELL, T., 21, 29, 49
BIDDLE, Hon. Edward, 20,
    39
BILLINGSLY, John, 40
BIRD, William, 39?
BLACK, William, 62
BOND, Betsy, 38
    John, 4
    Thomas, 20
BOOTH, Betsy, 60
    Priscilla, 50
BOUSH, John, 33
BOWEN, Jehu, 54
BOWIE, Fielder, 13
BOWLY, ---, 56

BOWMAN, Waltara, 16
BOYD, Jane, 58
BRERETON, Mrs. Sarah, 50
BRIDE, Polly, 3
BROOKE, Miss, 18
    Richard, 18
    Samuel, 44
BROTHERSON, Charles, 67
BROWN, G. R., 56
    Jacob, 47
BROWNING, Jeremiah, 10
BUCHANAN, ---, 9
    Gen., 38
    Dorothy, 38
    Polly, 1
    Sarah, 59
    William, 1
BURGESS, Benj., 24
BURKE, Michael, 8
BURLAND, Betsy, 13
    Richard, 13
BURLING, Mr., 15

CALHOUN, James, 42
CAMPBELL, Francis, 9
    Margaret, 29
CAREY, James, 58
CARNAN, Charles R., 10
CARROLL, Charles, 10
    Polly, 10
CASSIDY, Jane, 65
CAUSIN, Gerard B., 15
CHASE, Miss, 49
    J. T., 42
    Matilda, 49
    Hon. Samuel, 49
CHESLEY, John, 38, 58
    Rebecca, 58
    Robert, 38
CHEW, Miss, 31

CHEW, Benj., 31
    John, 24

CLAGGETT, Thomas, 26
CLAPHAM, John, 56
CLARK, James, 7
CLELAND, Samuel, 20
CLEMENTS, Betsy, 40
    Teresia, 12
CLINGAN, Miss, 53
    James, 53
COALE, P., 23
COCKEY, Joshua, 45
COE, William, 4
COLVIN, Priscilla, 52
CONRAD, Jacob, 42
COOK, Thomas, 53
COOPER, Rev., 55
COSTEN, Rebecca, 28
COUDEN, Rev. Joseph, 64
COURTENAY, Hercules, 43
CRADOCK, Thomas, 50
CRISMAN, Frederick, Sr., 57
CROCKETT, Betsey, 53
    James, 11
CUSRON, Richard, 58
CURSON, Richard, 58

DAVENPORT, ---, 16
DAVEY, Eliza, 19
DAVIDSON, John, 14
DAVIS, George, 25
    Robert Pain, 14
DAWSON, Widow, 28
    George, 9
DAY, Edward Fell, 20
    Isaac, 63
DEAL, Christian, 55
DE BUTTS, John, 54
DELOZIER, D., 63
DENNES, Capt. William, 56

INDEX

DENNY, R., 56
DIFFENDERFER, Mrs. Elizabeth, 3
  Michael, 41
DIGGES, George, 10, 21
DODD, John, 5
DODGE, Samuel, 1
DONALDSON, Joseph, 28, 60
DORSEY, Betsy, 60
  Betsy Goodwin, 52
  Charles of Nicholas, 19
  Edward, 31, 60
  Orlando G., 37
  Polly, 31
  William H., 12
DOWELL, Richard, 31
DOWSON, Joseph, 58
DRURY, Jerningham, 65
DUCHART, Peggy, 15
DUGAN, Cumberland, 2
DUKEHART, Betsy, 2
DUVALL, Alexander, 6
  G., 51
  Gabriel, 51
  Marsh M., 26, 33, 34

EDWARDS, James, 44
ELLICOTT, Elias, 24
  John, 10
  Patty, 10
ESTEP, Rezin, 33
EWING, Gen., 42
  Miss, 42

FAW, A., 51
FELL, William, 23
FENDALL, Dr. B., 31
  Philip R., 37
FERGUSON, Rev. Dr., 29
FINIATER, Alexander, 50
FINLAY, Hugh, 10
FLINT, Mrs. Margaret, 46
FORBES, John, 49
FORMAN, Ezekiel, 60
  Sally, 60

FORREST, Zachariah, 38
FOSTER, Jane, 49
FRANCISCUS, George, 60
FRICK, Peter, 21

GAITHER, Vachel, 21
GALE, John, 64
GALLION, Christian, 44
  Nathan, 44
GANTT, Thomas, 28
GEIGER, Susanna, 28
GEOGHEGAN, John, 62
GILLIATS, John, 27
  Thomas, 27
GILPIN, Hannah, 45
  Hon. Joseph, 45
GITTINGS, James, 14
  Nelly, 14
GOLDSMITH, W., 51
  William, 33
GORSUCH, Benjamin, 7
GOSZLER, Anthony, 64
GOUGH, Harry Dorsey, 10, 35
  Sophia, 10
GOULD, Capt. 37
GOULDING, Martha, 24
GRANT, Daniel, 26
  Jenny, 26
GRAVES, Miss, 14
  Col. Richard, 14
GRAY, John, 48
  Nancy, 48
  Samuel, 19
GRAYBILL, Philip, 51
  Polly, 51
GREEN, Frederick, 51
  Sarah, 12
  Vincent, 18

HAGER, John, 59
HAGERTY, John, Jr., 56
HAIFLIGH, Frederick, 3
HAIRS, David, 32
HALL, Aquila, 47
  Benedict E., 5
  Charlotte, 47

Elizabeth, 50
  George, 50
  John, 5
  Martha, 65
HAMBLETON, Mrs., 35
HAMMOND, Philip, 65
  William, 30, 31, 56
HANSON, Anna, 37
  Samuel, 37
HARMAN, Miss, 25
HARRIS, David, 42
  Frances, 42
HARRISON, Catharina, 59
  Joseph, II, 36
HARWOOD, Thomas, 34, 61
HASLETT, M., 8
HAWKSWORTH, Mary, 48
HAYES, James, 3
HAYMAN, John, 28
HAYWARD, John, 47
  W., 25
HEARD, James, 64
HELEMS, Joseph, 36
  Thomas, 36
HENDERSON, Philip, 41
  Rebecca, 41
HENRY, John, 8
  Isaac, 63
HESS, Jacob, 9
HEWITT, Caleb, 59
HEYSER, William, 39
HIGHJOE, Philip, 55
HILLEN, Solomon, 28
HINDMAN, Betsy, 9
  James, 1, 38
HOFFMAN, Peter, 2
HOLLIDAY, John Robert, 10, 59
HOLLINGSWORTH, Peggy, 12
  Zebulon, 12
HOPKINS, John, 59
  Peggy, 59
HOWARD, Joseph, 26
HUTTON, ---, 31

INGLETON, Edward, 59
IRELAND, Betsy, 30
  Edward, 30

JACOB, Samuel, 58
   Zachariah, 55
JACOBS, Hannah, 46
   William, 46
JAROLD, Betsy, 43
   Capt. Thomas, 43
JARVIS, John, 66
JOHNS, Thomas, 64
JOHNSON, Miss, 24
   Edward, 46
   Jeremiah, 54
   Josiah, 65
   Polly, 34
   Rebecca, 56
   Thomas, 24, 34
   William, 12, 56
JOHNSTON, Christopher, 16, 59
   Samuel, 28, 60
JONES, Robinson, 26
JUBIE, Mary, 62

KEENER, Christian, 65
   Melcher, 26
KEGY, Abraham, 35
KELLY, Patrick, 33
KELSO, James, 18
   Peggy, 18
KENT, Daniel, 33
KEPHART, David, 29
KERR, David, 23
KESLER, Adam, 13
KIMMERLY, John, 14
KNEASS, Hannah, 13

LANE, Betsy, 10
   Charlotte, 10
   Capt. Richard, 10, 15
   Samuel, 2
LARSCH, Abraham, 3, 46
   Valentine, 3
LATIMER, Ben, 56
LAWRENCE, Benjamin, 44
LEAMON, Jacob, 14
LEE, Pres., 62
   Alice, 62
   David, 1

   Hannah, 1
   Hon. Richard, 62
   Sarah Russell, 12
LEIGH, George, 50
LEMMON, Robert, 16
LEYPOLD, John, 60
LILLY, Peggy, 22
   Robert, 22
LIVINGSTON, Gov., 49
   Catherine, 49
LLEWELLIN, Charles, 19, 35
LLOYD, Mrs., 3
   Richard Bennett, 3
LONEY, Amos, 8
LONG, James, 42
LOUTTIT, James, 58
LUCE, Polly, 34
LUX, ---, 56
   Darby, 22
   George, 20, 66
   William, 22, 50

M'CASKEY, Polly, 13
M'CLELLAN, John, 13, 29
MACCUBBIN, Polly, 17
   Zachariah, 17
M'CULLOCH, J., 17
   Mary, 17
M'CREA, Rebecca, 1
   Robert, 1
McILHENEY, ---, 57
McINTIRE, Isabella, 43
   Thomas, 43
MACKALL, Levin, 13
M'KEAN, Letitia, 8
   Thomas, 8
MACKIE, Ebenezer, 3
MACKILVENE, Ann, 11
McKIRDY, Betsy, 32
   Capt. John, 32
McLAUGHLIN, William, 46
McQUINN, William, 18

MAGRUDER, John Read, 38
   W. B., 8
MARTIN, ---, 57

MATHERS, Capt. Joseph, 12
   Peggy, 12
MATTHEWS, George, 58
   Oliver, 32
   Peggy, 58
   Polly, 58
   W., 58
MAXWELL, Eliza, 57
   MARIAN, 9
   Nancy, 57
   Sally, 3
MEIGHAN, Mrs. Maria, 30
MESSERSMITH, Polly, 36
   Samuel, 36
MICKLE, Miss, 2
   John, 2, 42
MILES, Edward, 12
MILIARD, Joseph, 20
MITCHELL, John P., 31
MOALE, Frances, 28
   Richard, 28
MOORE, Susannah, 58
   William, 5
MORGAN, Nathaniel, 39
MOSS, James, 11
MURDOCKS, Eliza, 38
MURRAY, W., 21
MUSGROVE, Benjamin, 17

NEALE, Henry, 46
NELSON, Rebecca, 64
NEWCOMER, Christian, 9
NEWTON, Thomas, 33

NICHOLSON, Fanny, 52
   James, 52
NOBLE, Hetty, 58
NORWOOD, John, 40
NUTBROWN, Fanny, 32
   John, 32
   Sarah, 32

OLIVER, Rev. Mr., 23
O'NEALE, Lawrence, 10
ORNDORF, Conrad, 57
OWEN, Richard, 50
OWINGS, Samuel, 63

INDEX

PARKER, John, 16
PARKS, Betsy, 39
    John, 37, 39
    Jenny, 37
PATTERSON, William, 54
PEACHEY, Susanna, 43
    Col William, 43
PEARSON, Anne, 1
PENN, Benjamin D., 44
PENNINGTON, Josias, 27
PERKINS, Mr, 30
    Rachael, 30
PHELAN, Mary, 36
PILKINGTON, Mary, 65
    Thomas, 65
PLATER, George, 21
    Rebecca, 21
PLOWMAN, Jonathan, 40
    Polly, 40
POE, David, 42
POLE, Thomas Sam, 14, 62
POWNALL, Thomas, 16
PRATT, Frederick, 48
PURKINS, John, 28
PYPER, Thomas, 33

QUEEN, Joseph, 59
QUYNN, Allen, 16

RALPH, Nancy, 54
RANKIN, Polly, 27
    R, 27
REASE, George, 47
REEVES, Thomas Courtney, 13
REINECKER, George, 20
REITENAUER, Nicholas, 51
    Peggy, 51
RHODES, George Lester, 16
    Henry, 16
RICE, Nancy, 25
RIDLEY, Matthew, 52
RIDGELY, Richard, 31
RIGGEN, John, 28
RILEY, Barney, 5

RISTEAU, Fanny, 44
RITTER, Thomas, 43
ROBB, ---, 9
ROBERTS, Benjamin, 54
ROBINSON, Alexander, 5
    Priscilla, 5
RODNEY, Admiral, 16
ROE, Walter, 65
ROGERS, Miss, 6
    Benjamin, 6, 10
    Mary, 10
ROLE, Richard, 51
ROTHERY, Mary, 48
ROWLAND, Jane, 10
    William, 10
RULE, Sally, 45
RUMSEY, John, 33
RUSSELL, Wm, 22
RUTTER, Jonathan, 27
    Thomas, 48

SADLER, S., 36
SALMON, George, 20, 31
SAMPSON, Martha, 22
SANGSTOR, Nehemiah, 29
SCHOOLFIELD, William, 65
SCHWARTZ, Charles, 11
SCOTT, Abraham, 44
    Daniel, 12
    Helen, 54
SEARS, Col. Isaac, 55
    Rebecca, 55
SELLERS, Francis, 33
SELLMAN, John, 2
    Johnzee, 48
    Leonard, 22
SEWELL, Polly, 35
SHAEFFER, Baltzer, 41
SHERMAN, Conrad, 42
SHEWELL, John, 5
SHULTZ, John, 15
    Sukey, 15
SIM, Joseph, 28
    Robert, 35
SIMMONS, Jonathan, 22
SINGLETON, John, 17
SLATOR, Robert, 42

SMITH, Elizabeth, 12
    Jenny, 30
    John, 28, 30
    Peggy, 29, 54
    Samuel, 54
    Thoroughgood, 48
    William, 54
    Winnefred, 12
SPARROW, Solomon, 36
SPEAR, Jane, 21
    William, 21
SPRIGG, Joseph, 38
STANFORD, Richard, 55
STANSBURY, Jane, 67
STERLETT, John, 23
    Polly, 23
STEUART, C., 17
    Charles, 3
    David, 19
    William, 40
STEVENSON, Henry, 28
STODDARD, David, 17
STODDERT, Benjamin, 64
STONE, Walter, 18
STUART, Richardson, 10, 63
STULL, Mrs., 50
    Col. John, 50
STUMP, John, 32
SWEARINGEN, Thomas, 63
SWEETING, Frances, 38

TAYLOR, Nelly, 48
TEMPLE, Miss, 64
    Hon. John, 64
THOMAS, Evan, 24, 46
    John, 34
    Nancy, 46
    Peggy, 7
    Richard, 7
THOMPSON, Rev. Mr., 2
    Betsey, 2
    Clare, 12
    Dekar, 20
    John, 3
    Nancy, 3
THOMSON, Mrs., 1
    Andrew, 1

INDEX

TIBBITT, James, 21
   Sarah, 21
TILLY, Jasper Edward, 39
TINKER, William, 59
TOWNSAND, Henry, 64
TOWNSLEY, John, 34
TRICKLE, Polly, 26
TRIMBLE, William, 6
TROUTMAN, Michael, 53
TSCHUDY, Nicholas, 11
TURNER, Richard W , 61
   Samuel, 17
TYSON, Elisha, 1

USHER, Joseph, 28
   Thomas, 28
   Thomas, Jr., 28
   Thomas B., 28

VALIANCE, Mary, 22
VAN DYKE, Sally, 63
VAUGHAN, Christopher, 47
VENNUMS, Nathan, 8

WADE, Robert, 58
WALLACE, Capt., 53
   Sarah, 23
WALTERS, J., 54
WAREHAM, Rev R ader, 27
WARFIELD, Nicholas
   Ridgely, 2
WARMAN, William Berry, 4
WATERS, Ann, 66
   Nancy, 33
   Philip, 66
WATKINS, Nicholas, 60
WEATHERALL, Henry, 8
WEATHERBURN, John, 47
WEAVER, John, 42
WEDERSTRANDT, C. T., 4
WEEMS, David Locke, 33
   John, 40
WEHRLY, George, 3
WELCH, George, 54
   Rebecca, 15
WELLS, Cornelius, 55
   Cyprian, 24
WELSH, Hanutel, 27, 49
WHETCROFT, B., 51
WHITTINGTON, Rousby, 28
WIESENTHAL, Dr. Charles
   F., 41
WILEY, Richard, 32
WILLIAMS, Gen., 10, 57
   James, 18, 58
WILLIAMSON, D., 39
   Nancy, 46
   Polly, 57

WILMER, Rev Mr., 6
WILSON, James, 54
   Stephen, 16
WINCHESTER, Lydia, 42
   William, 42
WINNING, Margaret, 64
WINTER, John, 9
WORTHEY, Francis, 15
   Mary, 15
WORTHINGTON, Betsey, 64
   William, 64

YATES, Joshua, 15
   Thomas, 42, 43
YEISER, Engelhard, 21
YIELDHALL, Elizabeth, 49
YOUNG, Delilah, 6
   Elizabeth, 56
   John, 56
   Notley
   Susanna, 8